# Chess College 1: Strategy

## Efstratios Grivas

*Translated by Sotiris Logothetis*

First published in Greek language under the series title *Skakistiki Proponisi* by Kedros in 2004
First published in English language in the UK by Gambit Publications Ltd 2006

ISBN-13: 978-1-904600-45-9
ISBN-10: 1-904600-45-X

DISTRIBUTION:
Worldwide (except USA): Central Books Ltd, 99 Wallis Rd, London E9 5LN.
Tel +44 (0)20 8986 4854 Fax +44 (0)20 8533 5821. E-mail: orders@Centralbooks.com
USA: Continental Enterprises Group, Inc., 302 West North 2nd Street, Seneca, SC 29678, USA.

For all other enquiries (including a full list of all Gambit chess titles) please contact the publishers, Gambit Publications Ltd, 6 Bradmore Park Rd, Hammersmith, London W6 0DS, England.
E-mail: info@gambitbooks.com
Or visit the GAMBIT web site at http://www.gambitbooks.com

Edited by Graham Burgess
Typeset by John Nunn
Cover image by Wolff Morrow
Printed in Great Britain by The Cromwell Press, Trowbridge, Wilts.

**Dedications**
*To my children Katerina and Michalis, who are the source of my inspiration*
and
*To Sophie, my life's alter ego*

10 9 8 7 6 5 4 3 2 1

**Gambit Publications Ltd**
*Managing Director:* GM Murray Chandler
*Chess Director:* GM John Nunn
*Editorial Director:* FM Graham Burgess
*German Editor:* WFM Petra Nunn
*Webmaster:* WFM Helen Milligan

# Contents

Symbols                                                              4
Bibliography                                                         5

Introduction                                                         6
Getting to Know Ourselves                                            8
Training                                                            10
Attacking the Uncastled King                                       12
Attacking the King: Castling on the Same Side                      27
Attacking the King: Castling on Opposite Sides                     39
The Exchange Sacrifice                                             49
The Positional Sacrifice                                           61
Outpost                                                            69
Open File                                                          79
Semi-Open File                                                     92
Forepost                                                          102

Index of Games                                                    109
Index of Openings                                                 111

# Symbols

| | |
|---|---|
| + | check |
| ++ | double check |
| # | checkmate |
| !! | brilliant move |
| ! | good move |
| !? | interesting move |
| ?! | dubious move |
| ? | bad move |
| ?? | blunder |
| +– | White is winning |
| ± | White has a large advantage |
| $\pm$ | White is slightly better |
| = | equal position |
| $\mp$ | Black is slightly better |
| $\mp$ | Black has a large advantage |
| –+ | Black is winning |
| Ch | championship |
| Cht | team championship |
| Wch | world championship |
| Wcht | world team championship |
| Ech | European championship |
| Echt | European team championship |
| ECC | European Clubs Cup |
| tt | team event |
| jr | junior event |
| wom | women's event |
| OL | olympiad |
| rpd | rapidplay game |
| simul | game from simultaneous display |
| 1-0 | the game ends in a win for White |
| ½-½ | the game ends in a draw |
| 0-1 | the game ends in a win for Black |
| *(n)* | *n*th match game |
| *(D)* | see next diagram |

# Bibliography

*Informator*; various contributors; Informator 1966-2004
*Chess World Championships*; James H. Gelo; McFarland 1999
*ChessBase Mega Database*; various contributors; ChessBase 2004
*Encyclopaedia of Chess Endgames* (database); various contributors; Informator 2004
*Exploring the Endgame*; Peter Griffiths; A. & C. Black 1984
*Greek Chess Chronicles*; Triantafyllos Siaperas; GCF 1970-3
*Greek International Masters*; Efstratios Grivas; Skyfos 1986
*Moscow Chess Seminar*; Efstratios Grivas; Aegina 1989
*New In Chess* (Magazine); various contributors; Interchess BV 1984-2004
*New In Chess* (Yearbooks); various contributors; Interchess BV 1984-2004
*NicBase Database*; various contributors; Interchess BV 2004
*Pawn Endings*; Alexandar Tsvetkov; Chess Enterprises 1985
Personal notes and analysis; Efstratios Grivas; 1980-2004
*Rook Endgames*; Yuri Averbakh; Sportverlag Berlin 1988
*Shakhmatny Biulleten*; various contributors; Shakhmatny Biulleten 1985-95
*Zurich International Chess Tournament 1953*; David Bronstein; Dover 1979

# Introduction

Every chess-player who wishes to improve his level in the difficult subject of chess is obliged, first of all, to study methodically and understand the existing principles that govern the theory of the opening, middlegame and endgame.

Most chess-players focus more on the study of opening theory than other aspects of the game. The reasons are probably clear: opening theory is easier to learn and can provide immediate results, although this is based more on the opponent's ignorance than our own abilities. Even for a chess trainer, it is easier to teach some variations from this or that opening or a set of simple tactical motifs than to engross himself in the exposition of middlegame and endgame theory.

Yes, middlegame and endgame theory does exist. The great difficulty in approaching it lies in the fact that it does not follow absolute and clear-cut paths, but rather involves deep research in the ideas and logic by which specific types of positions are treated. Moreover, unlike opening theory, the theory of the middlegame and the endgame does not change rapidly based on modern developments and remains almost intact through the years.

In view of the above, any chess-player who wishes to follow a chess career or simply become a better player must refrain from the commonplace and assume a different approach. He must develop a good understanding of middlegame and endgame theory, so as to be able in his games to proceed in a proper way after his chosen opening has reached its conclusion. The chess-player can differentiate himself only in the opening; there, each one of us brings forth his own beliefs and convictions, and in general his own experiences and preferences. Objectively, no opening loses – but also no opening wins. The opening is just the beginning of the journey and serves to offer us a comfortable start. But to reach the end of this journey successfully we have to count on our knowledge and experience, as regards middlegame and endgame theory.

Endgame theory teaches us two fundamental issues. First, how to extract the maximum from a basic theoretical position with little material, where the experts (and practice comprising thousands of games) have reached definite conclusions. Second, the way in which we can handle an endgame, depending on the material remaining on the board, and the ideas and plans we should employ. This second issue is significantly more difficult to master because, apart from making full use of the first one (we must be aware of the possible outcomes of the endgame in question) it is greatly influenced by our experience and understanding, which are basically derived from the images and impressions we have from related positions. And, of course, a primary role is played by the effort we have invested in studying.

In middlegame theory, things are even tougher. We are obliged to study various types of positions with specific strategic and tactical attributes, so as to understand the underlying ideas and be able to employ them ourselves in similar situations. Besides, while many chess-players have studied these topics and acquired knowledge, it is the application of this knowledge in practice that helps differentiate between them. True, chess is not a simple activity, but it becomes so much more attractive when we acquire this knowledge...

This is the first of three books that deal with middlegame and general chess theory. The purpose of this series is to introduce the reader to advanced training concepts, using the same methods of presentation and instruction that were taught to me personally by famous trainers that I have worked with. I owe to these people gratitude for their valuable contribution to my progress as a chess-player. Besides, the fact that I succeeded in attaining the grandmaster title is owed first and foremost to the education I received and then to my personal work and effort.

## Volume 1: Strategy

In this book we look at training methods and general issues related to preparation for competitive play. We move on to discuss a number of major strategic themes, including the attack on the king, positional sacrifices, and various types of positional advantage.

# Getting to Know Ourselves

It is essential to become acquainted with ourselves chesswise so as to be able to identify and codify the assets and weaknesses of our chess personality. But how can this be done? Our basic source shall be the games we have played so far. We must re-examine this material and produce an 'X-ray' image of our chess self. This examination must include all three parts of the game, opening, middlegame and endgame, for each of our games.

Starting with the opening, we shall fill up two charts, one for the white and one for the black pieces. These charts will provide very clear-cut information about ourselves (provided of course that we do this work with strong self-criticism) and will show how well we understand the openings we have chosen or, in the bottom line, whether these openings really suit our style (difference between opening outcome and game result). The bigger the sample, the more accurate the conclusions.

| Opening Examination | | | | | | | | | |
|---|---|---|---|---|---|---|---|---|---|
| Games with White | | | | Opening outcome | | | Result of the game | | |
| | Opponent | Rating | Opening | + | = | − | 1 | ½ | 0 |
| 1 | | | | | | | | | |
| 2 | | | | | | | | | |
| 3 | | | | | | | | | |
| 4 | | | | | | | | | |
| 5 | | | | | | | | | |
| 6 | | | | | | | | | |
| 7 | | | | | | | | | |
| 8 | | | | | | | | | |
| 9 | | | | | | | | | |
| 10 | | | | | | | | | |
| | Totals | | | | | | | | |

Here is an example of how to fill in these charts:

| Opening Examination | | | | | | | | | |
|---|---|---|---|---|---|---|---|---|---|
| Games with White | | | | Opening outcome | | | Result of the game | | |
| | Opponent | Rating | Opening | + | = | − | 1 | ½ | 0 |
| 1 | Shirov | 2732 | Sicilian | | x | | | x | |
| 2 | Gelfand | 2690 | King's Indian | x | | | | x | |

Next, we shall move on to a similar chart in order to examine our performance in the middlegame. This chart will contain our games with both White and Black, and requires a sample of at least 40 games to produce reliable results.

| Middlegame Examination | | | | | | | | |
|---|---|---|---|---|---|---|---|---|
| Games with White & Black | | | Handling of the middlegame | | | Result of the game | | |
| | General type | Middlegame type | + | = | − | 1 | ½ | 0 |
| 1 | Strategy | Open position | | | | | | |
| 2 | | Semi-open position | | | | | | |
| 3 | | Closed position | | | | | | |
| 4 | Tactics | Attack against the king | | | | | | |
| 5 | | Defence of the king | | | | | | |
| 6 | | Combinative play | | | | | | |
| | Totals | | | | | | | |

An example of how to fill in the middlegame chart:

| Middlegame Examination | | | | | | | | |
|---|---|---|---|---|---|---|---|---|
| Games with White & Black | | | Handling of the middlegame | | | Result of the game | | |
| | General type | Middlegame type | + | = | − | 1 | ½ | 0 |
| 1 | Strategy | Open position | 4 | 2 | 0 | 5 | 0 | 1 |
| 2 | | Semi-open position | 2 | 3 | 3 | 3 | 2 | 3 |
| 3 | | Closed position | 0 | 3 | 3 | 0 | 0 | 6 |
| 4 | Tactics | Attack against the king | 5 | 0 | 0 | 5 | 0 | 0 |
| 5 | | Defence of the king | 1 | 0 | 4 | 1 | 1 | 3 |
| 6 | | Combinative play | 6 | 2 | 2 | 5 | 4 | 1 |
| | Totals | | 18 | 10 | 12 | 19 | 7 | 14 |

We shall then work similarly to create our endgame chart:

| Endgame Examination | | | | | | | |
|---|---|---|---|---|---|---|---|
| Games with White & Black | | Handling of the endgame | | | Result of the game | | |
| | Endgame Type | + | = | − | 1 | ½ | 0 |
| 1 | Pawn endgame | | | | | | |
| 2 | Queen endgame | | | | | | |
| 3 | Rook endgame | | | | | | |
| 4 | Bishop endgame | | | | | | |
| 5 | Knight endgame | | | | | | |
| 6 | Combinations of the above | | | | | | |
| | Totals | | | | | | |

After completing this work we will have a much clearer picture of both our weaknesses and our strengths. It is recommended to repeat this process at frequent intervals, provided of course that we have gathered enough material from recent games. In this way we can evaluate our improvement or discover other hidden aspects of ourselves.

# Training

Chess books and databases can be of valuable help to the progress of an ambitious chess-player. However, besides these indispensable tools, the role of the trainer is both significant and essential. This consideration immediately spawns a question: who is the indicated trainer?

An answer to this question does not come easily. Every trainer is useful in specific stages in the progress of a chess-player. We could try to categorize chess trainers as follows:

**First-Level Trainer:** The trainer who will teach the student the basics and bring him into contact with the world of chess. One of his main aims is to infuse the student with love and respect for chess.

**Second-Level Trainer:** The trainer who will teach the student his first openings, simple tactical motifs and, generally, will introduce the student to the aspects of working and learning.

**Third-Level Trainer:** The trainer who will teach the student, first and foremost, the theory of the middlegame and the endgame. Moreover, he will work closely with the student towards the creation of the student's personalized openings repertoire, which he will also help enrich with new ideas.

**Fourth-Level Trainer:** The trainer who will continue in the footsteps of the previous one, but will also introduce the student to other important aspects of chess, such as the concept of and preparation for competitive success. Trainers of such calibre and skill are very scarce, and are only necessary to those chess-players who wish to reach a high level of play or seek competitive success in any form.

## The Ideal Trainer

There are two main categories of chess-players. In the first one belong those who attain pleasure from the study of books, analysis and generally observe chess life 'from afar', without competing. In the second belong those who, without neglecting all the above, enjoy the direct fight, combining these aspects with the pleasure they draw from imposing their ideas and thoughts on those of the opponent.

The chess-player that permanently competes is genetically programmed to dominate and question authority. He is destined to compete, to compare, to become better than the next guy. He is worried about the 'natural end' and desperately seeks material gains and as much happiness as possible. Chess is a bloodless battle and the concept of peace is practically non-existent. And this is the constant vindication of Plato, who wrote in his *Laws* that "there is an undeclared and permanent war among everyone, imposed by some natural law, and the word *peace* is decorative".

It is true that someone may be destined to be a Hollywood star, a prince or a millionaire, just as it is true that nobody is destined to become a grandmaster. The accomplishment of this task requires hard and persistent work. One must have passion to climb the chess Olympus; otherwise it is a waste of time. Passion is uncontrollable; it comes from the soul, not the mind.

Strong chess-players, when they retire from competitive play, lack a natural career path. Most of them decide to disappear from the chess community, but some of them stick around and occupy themselves with the art of training. They are ready to convey their knowledge and experience, and are able to draw pleasure from the competitive and artistic achievements of those they have assisted.

The ideal trainer, the expert in the art of training, does not differentiate between work and play, job and pleasure, spirit and body, lesson and break, love and religion. He barely even knows which is which. He simply follows a vision of superiority, no matter what he is doing, leaving his students to determine when he is working and when he is playing. He himself is always doing both!

It is said that 'only gods and fallen angels are alone'. Great chess-players have never been gods, but they can have disciples.

We now move on to specific issues on the chessboard itself.

# Attacking the Uncastled King

Despite the significant advances made in defensive technique over the years, the phenomenon of the unprotected king is still quite common. By this we mean a king that has come under enemy fire and that is not readily repulsed.

There are two basic motivations behind castling:

1) The king is transferred to a safe place, away from immediate danger, waiting for an endgame to arise, in which the king can play an important role.

2) By its departure from the central files the king enables all the other pieces – particularly the rooks – to cooperate.

Around the start of the 20th century, attacks against an uncastled king were very common and often crowned with success, mostly due to complete ignorance of the defensive potential inherent in a position and the techniques to make use of it. Today, every chess-player is aware of and makes full use of such concepts, thus refuting aggressive ventures that do not fulfil 'basic requirements'. But what are these basic requirements necessary for an attack to succeed?

1) Superiority, either material or positional, on the sector of the board where the attack is to be carried out. By the term 'material superiority' we imply the more active placement and easy access of attacking forces to that sector and not necessarily an overall material advantage that has come about after capturing enemy pieces. This principle is of a very dynamic nature, as the material balance in one part of the board can easily be disturbed in the defender's favour by the successful transfer of defensive forces to that sector.

2) Lack of defensive pieces or pawns around the king to come under attack.

3) Control of the centre, or at least increased stability in that area. In most cases where this requirement is not met, the attack is doomed to fail.

An attack against an uncastled king can be carried out in several different ways. *As a rule, the main attacking methods are*:

1) Attack down the file where the target is temporarily situated; this is usually the e-file.

2) Attack via neighbouring squares protected only by the king; the most common such square is f7 (f2).

3) Prevention of castling, either permanent or temporary, so that the attack acquires a more or less permanent nature.

Naturally, meeting all the basic requirements is alone not enough to bring the desired result. The side attacking an uncastled king also faces some other obligations:

1) To open lines.

2) To transfer more forces to the relevant area in order to strengthen the attack.

3) To cause a further weakening of the opponent's defensive shield.

4) To avoid the exchange of potentially useful attacking pieces.

5) To exchange the opponent's potentially useful defensive pieces.

6) To focus on the attack against the opponent's king and not to be distracted by some irrelevant material gain.

On the other hand, the defender must also follow certain guidelines in order to fight successfully for survival:

1) To strengthen his king's defence.

2) To transfer the king to a safe place.

3) To switch, when appropriate, between active and passive defence.

4) To counterattack.

5) To evaluate the opponent's threats calmly and objectively. Launching an attack involves

certain concessions. These can be material (sacrifices) or positional (creation of permanent weaknesses, etc.). Thus, the attacking side must strike a balance between fuelling the attack and making as few such concessions as possible, so that a possible failure of the attack will not leave his position devastated. Naturally, this applies only while the final outcome of the attack is unclear; once it becomes clear that the opponent cannot defend successfully, further restraint is unnecessary.

Generally, every attack causes a more or less serious disturbance of the equilibrium, which is very rarely restored because the attacker often chooses to burn his bridges behind him.

### Grivas – Kjeldsen
*Cannes 1995*

**1 d4 ♘f6 2 c4 c5 3 d5 b5 4 ♗g5 g6 5 d6!?** *(D)*

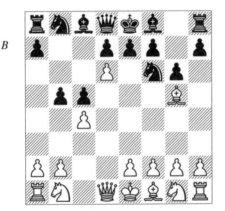

**5...bxc4!**

Other moves have fared worse: 5...exd6? 6 ♘c3! ♗e7 7 ♘xb5 0-0 8 ♘f3 ♗b7 9 ♘xd6 ♗xf3 10 gxf3 ♕b6 11 ♕d2! ± Grivas-Lputian, Athens 1983; 5...♗b7 6 ♗xf6 exf6 7 ♘c3 a6 8 ♕d2 ♘c6 9 cxb5 axb5?! 10 ♘xb5 ± Miles-Bellon, Surakarta/Denpasar 1983.

**6 ♘c3**

White ends up in a suspect position after the overambitious 6 ♗xf6?! exf6 7 ♕d5? ♕b6!!.

**6...♘c6**

Black's best option. Again the alternatives are unsatisfactory: 6...exd6?! (6...♗b7? 7 ♕d2! ♘e4 8 ♘xe4 ♗xe4 9 f3 ♗b7 10 e4 ±) 7 ♘e4

♗e7 (7...♕a5+? 8 ♗d2 ♕d8 9 ♘xf6+ ♕xf6 10 ♗c3) 8 ♘xd6+ ♔f8 (8...♗xd6? 9 ♕xd6 ♘e4 10 ♕e5+) 9 ♗xf6 ♗xf6 10 ♕d5 ♔g7! (10...♕a5+? 11 ♔d1 ♗e7 12 ♕xf7+! ♔xd6 13 ♕xf6+) 11 0-0-0! (Black is better after both 11 ♕xa8? ♕a5+ 12 ♔d1 ♕a4+ and 11 ♕xf7+? ♔h6 12 ♘f3 ♖f8! {12...♗xb2? 13 g4!! ♕a5+ 14 ♘d2 c3 15 g5+!} 13 0-0-0 ♗xb2+ 14 ♔c2 ♕f6!) 11...♕e7 (11...♘c6? 12 ♕xf7+ ♔h6 13 ♘f3) 12 e3!? (12 ♕xa8? ♘c6 13 ♘xc8 ♕e5! leaves Black better, but 12 ♘xc8! ♖xc8 13 ♕xa8 ♗xb2+ 14 ♔xb2 ♕f6+ 15 ♔b1 {not 15 ♔c2? ♘c6! 16 ♕xc8 ♘b4+} 15...♘c6 16 ♕xc8 ♕f5+ 17 e4 ♕xe4+ 18 ♗d3 cxd3 19 ♕b7 also wins) 12...c3!? (other moves also leave White clearly better: 12...♘c6 13 ♗xc4!; 12...♗a6 13 ♗xc4 ♗xc4 14 ♘xc4) 13 ♕xa8 (not 13 ♘xc8? ♖xc8 14 ♕xa8 c4!! 15 ♕b7 ♘c6!) 13...♘c6 14 ♘f3 c2 15 ♔xc2 ♗a6 (15...♕d8? 16 ♘f5+!? gxf5 17 ♕xc6) 16 ♕xc6!! and White's superiority is significant.

**7 ♕d2** *(D)*

Another interesting continuation is 7 e4!? h6 8 ♗e3! exd6 9 ♗xc4, with a slight advantage for White.

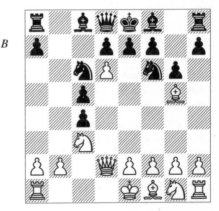

**7...♗g7**

Not, of course, 7...exd6? 8 ♕e3+!.

**8 e4**

8 dxe7?! ♕xe7! 9 ♘d5?! ♕e5! is good for Black.

**8...h6!**

If Black attempted to continue with 8...0-0?! 9 ♘f3 exd6 (9...♘d4 10 e5!) 10 ♗xc4 ♖e8 11 0-0 White would retain a pleasant initiative.

Note that Black cannot relieve the pressure with 11...h6? due to 12 ♗xh6 ♘xe4 13 ♘xe4 ♖xe4 14 ♗xf7+!.

**9 ♗f4!? g5!**

Black consistently fights for the advantage. Another possibility was 9...e5!? 10 ♗e3 ♘d4 11 ♗xc4 ♗b7 12 f3 0-0 (after 12...h5?! 13 ♗g5! White dominates the d5-square) 13 ♗xh6! ♘c2+ 14 ♕xc2 ♗xh6 15 ♕d3 with an unclear position.

**10 ♗e3** *(D)*

Once again the capture on e7 is unsatisfactory: 10 dxe7? ♕xe7 11 ♗d6 ♘xe4!.

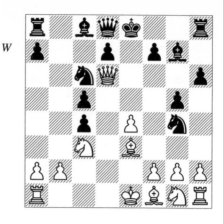

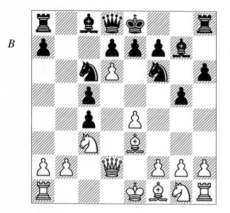

**10...exd6?!**

Up to this point Black has avoided all pitfalls but here, driven by the desire to extinguish White's initiative, he 'forgot' about the importance of castling – or assumed that he will be able to accomplish it soon! It is true that 10...♘g4?! 11 ♗xc5 ♕a5 12 ♗a3 would also not equalize, but Black should have played 10...♕a5! 11 ♗xc4 ♘g4 12 dxe7 (12 ♘f3? ♘xe3 13 fxe3 e6!) 12...♘xe3 13 fxe3 ♗xc3! 14 ♕xc3 (14 bxc3? ♘e5 15 ♗d5 ♖b8 16 ♘f3?! ♖b2!) 14...♕xc3+ 15 bxc3 ♘e5 16 ♗d5 ♖b8 17 ♘f3 ♘d3+ (17...f6? 18 ♘xe5 fxe5 19 0-0 is good for White) 18 ♔d2 ♗a6 19 ♖ab1 ♔xe7 with balanced chances.

**11 ♕xd6 ♘g4?** *(D)*

The decisive mistake! Black was compelled to play 11...♘d4! 12 ♖c1! (12 ♗xd4? cxd4 13 ♕xd4 0-0 is great for Black) 12...♕b6 13 ♕xb6 axb6 14 ♗xc4 ±.

**12 ♗xc4!**

Instead, 12 ♗xc5? ♕a5 13 ♘e2 ♗f8 would be equivalent to resignation.

**12...♘xe3 13 fxe3 ♕a5**

White retains his superiority after 13...♗xc3+ 14 bxc3 ♕e7 15 ♕d5 intending ♘e2-g3.

**14 ♘e2 ♘e5**

14...♗e5 is no improvement: 15 ♕d5 0-0 16 0-0 ±.

**15 ♗d5! ♘d3+ 16 ♔d2 ♘xb2?!**

This eases White's task. Black should have tried 16...♗e5!?, when after 17 ♗xf7+ ♔xf7 18 ♕xd3 d6! 19 ♕d5+ ♗e6 20 ♖hf1+ ♔e7 21 ♕b7+ ♗d7, White would have to find the spectacular 22 b4!! (22 ♖f7+? is just a draw) 22...cxb4 (or 22...♕xb4 23 ♖f7+! ♔xf7 24 ♕xd7+ ♔g6 25 ♖b1! with an easy win for White; 22...♕d8 23 ♘d5+ ♔e6 24 ♘c7+) 23 ♘d5+ ♔e6 24 ♘d4+! (and not 24 ♖f7? b3+! 25 ♔d1 ♔xf7 =) 24...♗xd4 25 exd4 ♖af8 26 ♕xb4 ±.

**17 ♖hf1 ♖f8 18 ♖ab1!** *(D)*

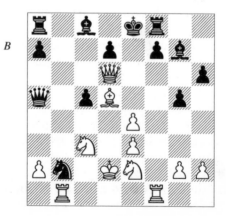

All of White's pieces occupy very active positions, while their black counterparts are unable to create any serious threats.

**18...♘a4**

White had no reason to worry about 18...♕a3 19 ♔c2 ♘a4 20 ♖b3! or 18...♕b4 19 ♔c2 ♖b8 20 a3!, with a winning position in both cases.

**19 e5!**

The black a8-rook is of relatively minimal value. Indeed, 19 ♗xa8? ♗xc3+! 20 ♘xc3 ♕xc3+! would only be unclear at best.

**19...♘b6 20 ♖xb6!**

Eliminating Black's only active piece.

**20...axb6 21 ♘g3!** *(D)*

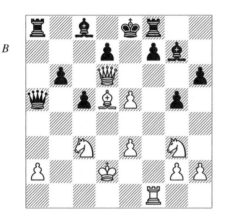

The complications have obviously ended in White's favour. In a *quantitative assessment* of the position Black is currently ahead in material. But in terms of a *qualitative assessment* White's pieces are much better placed and directed against a specific target (the black king on e8). This game is a characteristic case where Black ignored the necessity of safeguarding his king in favour of other priorities. As a result, the king has ended up surrounded by the white forces, while all of Black's active pieces have left the board!

**21...f5**

Desperation, but other moves also bring no salvation: 21...♖h8 22 ♘f5 ♗f8 23 ♕f6 ♖h7 24 ♗xf7+ ♖xf7 25 ♘d6+ ♗xd6 26 ♕xf7+ ♔d8 27 exd6; 21...♕a3 22 ♘f5 c4 23 ♘xg7+ ♔d8 24 ♕xb6+ ♔e7 25 ♕f6#.

**22 exf6 ♖xf6 23 ♖xf6 ♕b4 24 ♘f5 ♕b2+ 25 ♔d1 1-0**

## Grivas – Szkudlarek
*Dortmund 1991*

**1 c4 f5 2 ♘c3 ♘f6 3 g3 g6**

3...d6 and 3...e5 seem preferable.

**4 ♗g2 ♗g7 5 e4!?** *(D)*

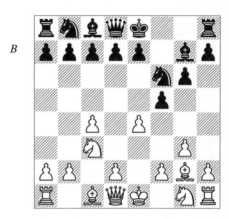

**5...fxe4**

Here 5...e5 6 d4! d6 7 dxe5 dxe5 8 ♕xd8+ ♔xd8 9 b3! leaves White with a considerable advantage.

**6 ♘xe4 ♘xe4?!**

Black should have accepted the slightly worse position which would arise after 6...0-0 7 d4.

**7 ♗xe4 e5**

7...0-0 is rather risky due to 8 h4!, while 7...e6 is interesting, though after 8 h4! d5 9 cxd5 exd5 10 ♗c2 White retains the initiative.

**8 h4 ♕f6 9 d3! ♖f8?!**

Black rejected 9...0-0 10 ♘h3, intending ♗g5, but he is surely not entitled to expect anything better with his king in the centre.

**10 ♗e3!**

The careless 10 ♘h3? d5! 11 ♗g5 ♕b6! 12 ♗e3 ♕b4+! 13 ♗d2 ♕b6 would force White to acquiesce to the repetition of moves.

**10...♘c6 11 ♘f3 d6 12 ♘g5! ♖h8 13 h5**

White has obtained a significant advantage due to his kingside initiative and the weakness of the pawn-chain g6-h7. Black's defensive potential is seriously in doubt.

**13...♗f5?!** *(D)*

13...♗d7 is much better, although White has the good reply 14 ♗d5! (not 14 ♘xh7? ♖xh7 15 ♗xg6+ ♕xg6).

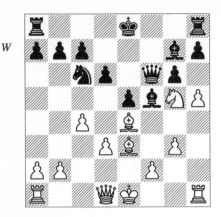

**14 h6! ♗f8 15 ♗xc6+!**

Not the immediate 15 ♕f3?! in view of 15...♘d4!.

**15...bxc6 16 ♕f3!**

The point of White's play initiated by 14 h6!. Now both 17 ♕xc6+ and 17 g4 are threatened.

**16...♔d7**

White wins after 16...♔e7 17 ♕xc6 ♖c8 18 0-0-0, intending ♘e4 and d4.

**17 g4 e4! 18 dxe4 ♕xb2 19 0-0**

Black has managed to retain material parity, but at the cost of leaving his king in the centre. White is far ahead in development, both in terms of quantity and quality, and now sets his sights on the usual target: the black king.

**19...♗e6 20 ♖fd1 ♕e5!** *(D)*

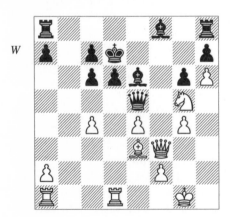

Smart defence by Black. If White now becomes greedy with 21 ♗d4? ♕xg5 22 ♗xh8 ♗xh6 Black will have succeeded in exchanging a superbly placed piece (g5-knight) for a useless rook (on h8) and White will have surrendered his initiative. This is one more example of the relative value of the pieces, a concept prevalent in the modern perception of evaluating a position.

**21 ♗f4! ♕c5 22 e5**

Opening lines. The black king is already feeling draughty!

**22...♗e7**

22...d5 23 ♖ac1! ♕a5 24 ♘xe6 ♔xe6 25 cxd5+ cxd5 26 ♖c6+ is of no help.

**23 ♘e4 ♕xc4 24 ♖ac1 ♕xa2 25 exd6 cxd6 26 ♗xd6 ♗d5 27 ♗xe7 1-0**

Black resigned due to 27...♔xe7 28 ♕f6+ ♔d7 29 ♕xc6+.

## Grivas – Siebrecht
*Budapest 1994*

**1 d4 d5 2 c4 c6 3 ♘f3 ♘f6 4 ♘c3 dxc4 5 e3 b5 6 a4 ♕a5?!** *(D)*

A dubious move. 6...b4 is more natural, when White can choose between 7 ♘a2 and 7 ♘b1.

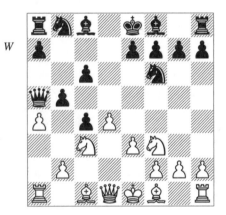

**7 ♗d2 b4**

7...♕b6 8 axb5 cxb5 9 b3! would also leave White better.

**8 ♘a2 e6 9 ♗xc4**

White is now targeting the black b4-pawn. Black will have to spend precious time eliminating one of the white pieces attacking this pawn.

**9...♘e4 10 0-0 ♘d7 11 ♘c1!**

White improves the placement of his knight, setting his sights on the important squares e5, c5 and a5.

**11...♗d6 12 ♗d3!**

Less accurate is 12 ♘b3?! ♕h5! 13 ♗d3 ♘g5!, when Black has a satisfactory game.

**12...♘xd2 13 ♘xd2 ♕c7**

This move shows the futility of 6...♕a5. It is true that Black now 'wins a tempo', but the queen is exposed on the semi-open c-file and will have to move again soon, thus returning the tempo...

**14 f4!** *(D)*

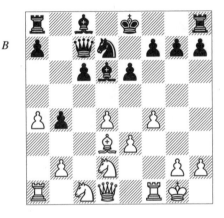

B

**14...c5?!**

Black should have resigned himself to an inferior position by 14...0-0 15 ♘cb3 ♗b7 16 ♖c1. In his efforts to achieve equality by drastic means, Black neglects the safety of his king. Naturally, opening up the position can in no way be to his benefit!

**15 ♘cb3 cxd4**

Practically forced. After 15...0-0? 16 ♖c1 White's advantage is decisive.

**16 ♘xd4 ♗b7**

Again after 16...0-0? 17 ♖c1 ♕b8 (17...♕d8 loses immediately to 18 ♗e4) 18 ♗e4 ♗b7 19 ♕f3! ♗xe4 20 ♘xe4 ♗e7 21 ♘c6 ♕e8 22 ♖c2! White has a large advantage.

**17 ♖c1! ♕d8** *(D)*

Other moves would meet the same fate: 17...♘c5? 18 ♗e4 a6 19 ♘4b3; 17...♕b8 18 ♗b5!.

It is clear that Black needs just one move (...0-0) to solve his problems almost in their entirety. Indeed, his position is free of static weaknesses, so White is obliged to act immediately if he wishes to benefit from his promising position.

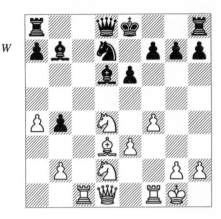

W

**18 ♗e4! ♗xe4**

18...♖b8 is no better: 19 ♕f3! ♗a8 20 ♗xa8 ♖xa8 21 ♘c6.

**19 ♘xe4 ♗e7 20 ♘c6 ♕b6 21 ♘d6+ ♔f8 22 ♘xf7!**

A conclusive small combination, the direct result of White's positional and tactical superiority.

**22...♔xf7 23 ♕xd7 ♖he8**

23...♕xe3+ 24 ♔h1 ♖he8 25 ♘e5+ ♔f8 26 ♕xe6 is also losing for Black.

**24 f5!**

Opening more lines towards the black king.

**24...♕xe3+**

Of course if 24...exf5? White mates with 25 ♖xf5+ ♔g6 26 ♘e5+ ♔h6 27 ♖h5+!.

**25 ♔h1 exf5 26 ♖ce1 1-0**

### Grivas – Lagopatis
*Serres 1990*

**1 d4 d6 2 e4 ♘f6 3 f3 e5 4 d5 ♗e7**

Theory also suggests 4...g6 here. On the other hand, the over-ambitious continuation 4...♘xe4? 5 fxe4 ♕h4+ 6 ♔d2 ♕xe4 7 ♘c3 ♕g6 8 ♕f3!, Grivas-Giaidzi, Kavala (Balkaniad) 1990, is quite bad.

**5 ♗e3 ♘h5!?** *(D)*

An interesting idea. A standard line is 5...0-0 6 ♕d2 c6 7 c4 b5! 8 ♘c3! b4 9 ♘d1 with complex play, Korchnoi-P.Nikolić, Barcelona 1989.

**6 ♘e2!**

Instead, 6 ♕d2?! h6! would relieve Black because White cannot avoid the exchange of dark-squared bishops after ...♗g5.

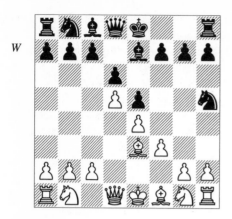

W

**6...$\unicode{x2657}$g5 7 $\unicode{x2657}$f2 g6!**

Intending to grab the initiative with ...0-0 and ...f5. White must react quickly.

**8 h4! $\unicode{x2657}$h6 9 g4 $\unicode{x2658}$f4 10 g5 $\unicode{x2657}$g7 11 $\unicode{x2658}$bc3 h6?**

Despite the fact that Black wins a pawn after this move, he will fall behind in development and encounter serious problems because of this. A better choice was 11...$\unicode{x2658}$d7 12 $\unicode{x2655}$d2 $\unicode{x2658}$xe2 13 $\unicode{x2657}$xe2 (13 $\unicode{x2655}$xe2!?) 13...h5! with White enjoying a slight advantage. Another interesting line is 11...$\unicode{x2658}$xe2 12 $\unicode{x2655}$xe2 h6 13 gxh6! $\unicode{x2657}$xh6 14 h5! gxh5 15 $\unicode{x2657}$e3, with White's initiative compensating for the pawn.

**12 $\unicode{x2658}$xf4! exf4 13 $\unicode{x2657}$d4** *(D)*

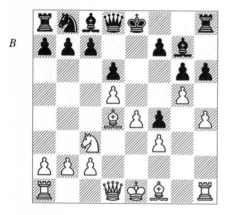

B

**13...$\unicode{x2657}$e5**

Other moves are no better: 13...f6 14 $\unicode{x2656}$g1!; 13...$\unicode{x2654}$f8 14 $\unicode{x2657}$xg7+ $\unicode{x2654}$xg7 15 $\unicode{x2655}$d4+ f6 16 $\unicode{x2656}$g1!.

**14 $\unicode{x2657}$xe5 dxe5 15 gxh6!**

This was compulsory. After 15 $\unicode{x2656}$g1? hxg5 16 hxg5 $\unicode{x2656}$h5 the pawn would be lost for practically no compensation.

**15...$\unicode{x2656}$xh6 16 $\unicode{x2655}$d2 $\unicode{x2656}$xh4?!**

If Black had taken White's next move into account he would surely have given more consideration to 16...$\unicode{x2658}$d7 17 0-0-0 $\unicode{x2658}$f6 18 $\unicode{x2657}$c4 a6 19 d6! $\unicode{x2655}$xd6 20 $\unicode{x2655}$xd6 cxd6 21 $\unicode{x2656}$xd6 $\unicode{x2654}$e7 22 $\unicode{x2656}$b6!, when White is 'merely' better.

**17 0-0-0!!** *(D)*

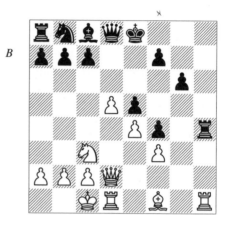

B

Completing White's development with the use of tactics.

**17...$\unicode{x2657}$d7**

Of course the rook was immune: 17...$\unicode{x2656}$xh1? 18 $\unicode{x2657}$b5+ c6 19 $\unicode{x2656}$xh1 +–.

**18 $\unicode{x2657}$c4 $\unicode{x2658}$a6 19 $\unicode{x2655}$f2!**

An excellent move, attacking the h4-rook, controlling c5 and secretly eyeing a7! The black king will have great difficulty finding a safe shelter and will consequently succumb to White's superior forces.

**19...$\unicode{x2656}$xh1 20 $\unicode{x2656}$xh1 $\unicode{x2655}$f6 21 $\unicode{x2657}$xa6 bxa6 22 d6!**

This advance splits Black's camp in two. Now 22...cxd6? 23 $\unicode{x2658}$d5 is disastrous for Black.

**22...c6 23 $\unicode{x2658}$a4!**

All of White's pieces rush to their most coveted squares. Black has no choice now.

**23...g5 24 $\unicode{x2658}$c5 0-0-0** *(D)*

It appears that Black has been relieved of his problems since he finally managed to castle and you may already be wondering why this game was included in this chapter. However, what we have here is a case of *deceptive*

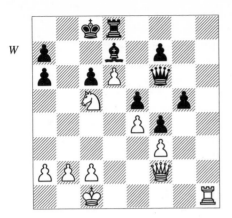

*king safety*. Indeed, Black's king is in no way secure in his new home, since he is lacking all the required prescriptions (healthy pawn-cover, defensive pieces, etc.). In fact, there is no essential difference between the previous and new situation of the black king – the hunt goes on!

**25 ♕d2!**

Threatening 26 ♕b4 or 26 ♕a5 with an almost certain mate. Instead, 25 ♕e2 ♚b8 26 ♕xa6? (26 ♕c4!) would prove totally misguided as after 26...♗c8 27 ♕xc6 ♕xd6 Black is better.

**25...♖h8 26 ♖d1 ♕d8**

To defend with 27...♕b6.

**27 ♕c3!**

Attacking the black e5-pawn, which cannot be successfully supported.

**27...♕b6**

If 27...f6 or 27...♖e8 there follows 28 ♕c4! ♕b6 29 ♘xd7 ♚xd7 30 ♕(x)f7+.

**28 ♘xd7 ♚xd7 29 ♕xe5** *(D)*

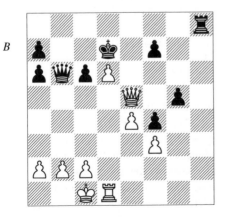

The material balance has been restored, but the black king has failed to find a shelter. Despite several exchanges, White's threats remain just as powerful as before.

**29...♕d8 30 ♕f5+ ♚e8 31 e5!?**

White could also win with 31 d7+ ♚f8 32 ♕c5+ ♚g7 33 ♕xc6, but with such a powerful position he feels entitled to seek even more.

**31...♖h6 32 ♖g1 ♕b6?!**

A time-trouble error, but the result was not in any doubt. 32...♖g6 loses to 33 ♖h1!.

**33 ♕c8+ ♕d8 34 ♕xc6+ ♚f8 35 ♕xa6 ♖e6 36 ♕d3 ♖xe5 37 ♖h1 ♖e8 38 ♕d4 f6**

Here Black lost on time, but of course 39 d7 wins immediately.

**1-0**

### Grivas – Kotronias
*Athens 1982*

**1 d4 ♘f6 2 c4 c5 3 d5 e6 4 ♘c3 exd5 5 cxd5 d6 6 ♘f3 g6 7 e4 ♗g7 8 ♗g5 h6 9 ♗h4 g5?!**

Too ambitious. The main line here is 9...a6 10 ♘d2 b5 with complex play.

**10 ♗g3 ♘h5 11 ♗b5+! ♚f8** *(D)*

Compulsory. After the natural-looking move 11...♗d7? Black ends up in a very bad position: 12 ♗xd7+ ♕xd7 13 ♘e5! ♕e7! 14 ♕xh5 ♗xe5 15 ♗xe5 ♕xe5 16 0-0.

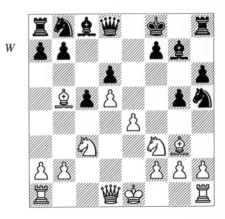

**12 ♗e2?!**

A bit too reserved! Best in this position is 12 e5! ♗g4 (12...g4 13 0-0!! ♘xg3 14 fxg3 dxe5 15 ♘h4 with an unstoppable attack, Grivas-Kondou, Athens 1983) 13 0-0! dxe5 (13...♘xg3

14 fxg3 ♗xe5 15 ♘xe5!! ♗xd1 16 ♘xf7! ♕b6 17 ♘xh8+ ♔g8 18 ♖axd1 ♔xh8 19 ♖f8+ ♔g7 20 ♖df1 is winning for White) 14 h3 ± Grivas-V.Peicheva, Primorsko 1989.

**12...♘xg3 13 hxg3 ♘d7 14 ♕c2 ♕e7**

Black dominates the dark squares and, overall, his position is safe and without serious weaknesses. Black's only concern is the somewhat unfortunate placement of his king, but White has no way of exploiting this at the moment. The position is dynamically balanced.

**15 ♘d1! ♘e5 16 ♘e3?!**

16 ♘d2, intending f3, g4 and ♘e3, controlling the important squares c4 and f5, should be preferred.

**16...♘g4!?** *(D)*

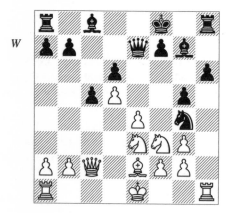

**17 0-0!?**

This is better than 17 ♘c4? b5! 18 ♘a5 ♕c7 19 ♘c6 b4 ∓, while 17 ♘xg4 ♗xg4 18 ♘g1! ♗xe2 19 ♘xe2 ♗f6 20 g4 ♗e5! is only equal. With the text-move, White accepts definite organic weaknesses, for which he hopes to compensate with a direct attack against the black king.

**17...♘xe3?**

Black had absolutely no reason to allow White any attacking chances and should instead have maintained the general character of the position with, for example, 17...♗f6.

**18 fxe3 ♗d7?!** *(D)*

And now 18...♗g4 ought to have been preferred. After 19 ♘h4! gxh4 20 ♗xg4 hxg3 21 ♗e6! ♗f6 (21...♕h4? 22 ♖xf7+ ♔e8 23 ♕a4+) 22 e5! dxe5 23 ♖xf6! ♕xf6 24 ♖f1 ♕xf1+

(24...♕h4? 25 ♖xf7+ ♔e8 26 ♕g6! ♕h2+ 27 ♔f1 ♕h1+ 28 ♔e2 ♕xg2+ 29 ♖f2+) 25 ♔xf1 fxe6 26 ♕xc5+ ♔f7 27 ♕c7+ ♔f6 28 d6 White has the initiative, but Black retains decent chances of salvation.

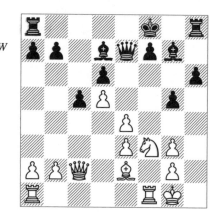

It is clear that the h8-rook will not be able to enter the battle any time soon, thus guaranteeing White a qualitative advantage of one rook. It is also obvious that the black king is not safe any more and Black will have to spend some time improving its shield. These factors favouring White are not static, while on the other hand Black's advantages (better pawn-structure, two bishops) are. Consequently, White must react immediately, as otherwise he will be doomed to a slow but certain defeat.

**19 e5!! dxe5**

Black would not fare any better by playing 19...♗xe5 20 ♘xe5, and now:

a) 20...♕xe5 21 ♗h5! ♕xe3+ (or 21...f5 22 e4! ♔g7 23 exf5 and then 23...♕f6 24 ♖ae1 ♖hf8 25 ♔h2 ♔g8 26 ♖e6! ♗xe6 27 fxe6 ♕g7 28 ♗f7+ ♔h8 29 ♕e2 or 23...♖hf8 24 f6+ ♖xf6 25 ♖xf6 ♕xf6 26 ♖f1 ♕d4+ 27 ♔h2) 22 ♔h2 ♗e8 23 ♖xf7+! ♗xf7 24 ♖f1 ♕e7 25 ♕g6.

b) 20...dxe5 21 ♗h5 ♗e8 22 ♖xf7+! ♗xf7 23 ♖f1 ♖d8 (23...♖e8? 24 ♕g6) 24 ♖xf7+ ♕xf7 25 ♗xf7 ♔xf7 26 ♕f5+ with a clear advantage for White.

**20 ♘d2!**

White regroups his pieces and opens files! The immediate intention is ♘e4, attacking the squares f6, d6 and c5.

**20...♔g8 21 ♘e4 f5?!** *(D)*

Black tries to gain some space but ultimately only succeeds in further weakening his kingside. Better is 21...b6 22 g4! ♖f8 23 ♖f2 and White is much better.

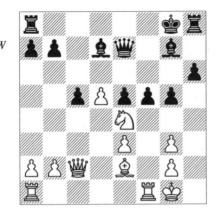

**22 ♗c4!**

And not the direct 22 d6?! ♕e8 23 ♗c4+ ♗e6. *The threat is stronger than its execution!*

**22...♔h7 23 d6 ♕e8 24 ♘xc5**

Materially the two sides are on equal terms now, but White's initiative keeps growing in all directions, and not necessarily only towards the black king.

**24...e4 25 ♕b3!**

Threatening 26 ♘xd7 ♕xd7 27 ♗e6, while the b7-pawn is also welcome!

**25...♖f8 26 ♕xb7 ♖d8**

Practically forced. There is no better solution: 26...♗c6? 27 d7! +–; 26...♕c8 27 ♕xc8! ♖fxc8 28 ♗d5 ♗b5 29 ♖xf5! ♖xc5 30 ♗xa8 ♖xf5 31 ♗xe4 +–.

**27 ♕xa7** *(D)*

White's overall superiority has now been crowned with material gain. Black essentially failed to defend, as he managed to safeguard his king only at great material cost. From now on Black tries to complicate the position, hoping to benefit from possible mistakes that White may make, either due to premature relaxation (he has a winning position) or to time-pressure.

In summary, White 'cashed in' his strong threats against the black king for material gain.

**27...♗e5!? 28 ♗b5! ♖f7 29 ♘xd7 ♖dxd7 30 ♗xd7 ♖xd7 31 ♕c5! ♖xd6 32 ♖xf5 ♗xg3**

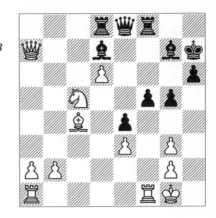

**33 ♖af1 ♕e6 34 b4 ♔g6 35 a4 ♔h5 36 ♕c2 ♕e7 37 b5 ♖d3 38 ♖f6! ♕g7**

38...♖xe3 allows mate after 39 ♕d1+ g4 40 ♖1f5+ ♔h4 41 ♖xh6#.

**39 b6! ♖xe3 40 b7 ♗e5 41 ♕f2! 1-0**

A possible finish to the game was 41...♖b3 42 ♕e2+ g4 43 ♖6f5+ ♔h4 44 ♕xe4 ♗d4+ 45 ♔h1 ♖xb7 46 ♕e1+ followed by mate in a few moves.

Naturally, things do not always need to be as disastrous as in the previous examples. To every action there is a reaction, to every attack there is a defence: sometimes obvious, sometimes hidden deep beneath the surface. The truth is: *he who searches, finds!*

## Wells – Grivas
*Reykjavik 1994*

**1 e4 c5 2 ♘f3 ♘c6 3 ♗b5 d6 4 0-0 ♗d7 5 ♖e1 ♘f6 6 c3 a6 7 ♗xc6**

A very sharp line, where White sacrifices material in the fight for the initiative. The alternatives 7 ♗f1 (Psakhis-Grivas, Tel-Aviv 1991) and 7 ♗a4 (Zhang Zhong-Grivas, Elista OL 1998) lead to quieter positions.

**7...♗xc6 8 d4 ♗xe4 9 ♗g5 ♗d5!?** *(D)*

Black has other options here, such as 9...d5, 9...♗xb1, and 9...♗xf3.

**10 ♘bd2**

10 c4!? is the sharpest move, but sacrificing two pawns in just ten moves constitutes a very heavy commitment.

**10...e6 11 c4 ♗xf3 12 ♕xf3 cxd4! 13 ♗xf6**

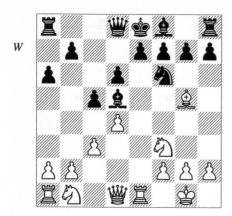

White can also try 13 ♕xb7 ♕c8! 14 ♕b6 (or 14 ♕f3 ♗e7 15 ♘b3 h6! 16 ♗h4 0-0 17 ♕d3! with equality) 14...♕c5 = Timoshchenko-Kupreichik, Ashkhabad 1978.

**13...gxf6 14 ♕xb7 ♗g7! 15 ♕c6+**

15 ♖xe6+?! fxe6 16 ♕xg7 ♖f8 17 ♕xh7 ♖c8, as in Buchal-Ribli, Bundesliga 1989/90, is not good for White.

**15...♔e7! 16 ♘b3 (D)**

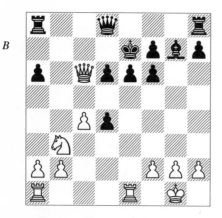

The black king has been 'self-imprisoned' in the centre, but White's attack has run out of steam. Thanks to the central pawn-mass, the black king is adequately protected, while the reduced material does not help White. Moreover, Black's minor piece (bishop vs knight) will prove superior in any endgame. White will most likely capture Black's temporary extra pawn. In view of all this, the position is unclear and dynamically balanced, though I tend to prefer Black.

**16...f5 17 ♖ad1 ♕c8!**

Black would welcome a transition to an ending. If now 18 ♕xc8?! ♖hxc8 19 ♘xd4 ♔d7! 20 b3 ♖c5 Black has a small but permanent plus.

**18 ♕f3?!**

Best was 18 ♕d5! ♗e5!? 19 ♖xe5 dxe5 20 ♕xe5 ♕b8! 21 ♕xd4 ♖d8 22 ♕h4+ ♔e8, with White retaining compensation for the material.

**18...♕xc4! (D)**

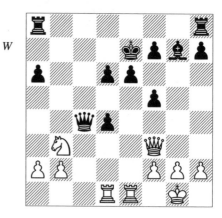

Brave, but at the same time also compulsory! Without this move Black's position would be very unpleasant.

**19 ♖c1?**

An 'easy' but ineffective move. I believe that White should have gone down the following line: 19 ♕xf5 ♖ac8 20 ♕g4 ♖hg8 21 ♘xd4 ♗xd4 22 ♕xd4 ♕xd4 23 ♖xd4 ♖c2 24 ♖b4 ♖g5! ∓. Of course, when viewed from a practical angle, it is not easy for White to admit the error of his ways and accept a transition to an inferior ending!

**19...♕b4! 20 ♖c7+**

Equally bad is 20 a3 ♕b8, when the b3-knight has lost its firm support.

**20...♔f6! 21 ♖f1**

A sad square for the rook, but the alternative 21 ♖ec1 ♖ac8! (exploiting the weakness of White's back rank) 22 a3 (22 ♖xc8 ♖xc8 23 ♖xc8 ♕e1#; 22 g3 ♖xc7 23 ♖xc7 ♕e1+ 24 ♔g2 ♕e4) 22...♕b8 would not improve White's critical situation.

**21...h5**

Defending against White's threat of 22 ♕h5.

**22 a3 ♕a4** *(D)*

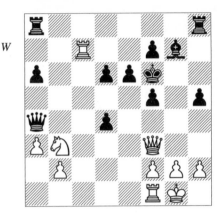

Preventing the activation of the white knight, while at the same time preparing ...♖ab8. White's position is desperate because he has failed to *coordinate his pieces*, while Black is utilizing his extra material to defend his king. The position does not offer White any hope for survival any more and all that is required from Black is some care and accuracy!

**23 ♘d2 d5! 24 ♕f4?**

A blunder in a lost position.

**24...♗h6! 25 ♕d6 ♗xd2 26 ♕e7+ ♔e5!**

The black king is perfectly safe in the centre of the board.

**27 ♖d7**

27 ♕xf7 ♕e8 28 ♕g7+ (or 28 f4+ ♔e4!) 28...♔d6 would not change anything.

**27...♖h7 28 ♕d6+ ♔f6 0-1**

### Collin – Grivas
*Belfort 1983*

**1 e4 e5 2 ♘f3 ♘c6 3 ♗b5 a6 4 ♗a4 ♘f6 5 0-0 ♘xe4 6 d4 b5 7 ♗b3 d5 8 dxe5 ♗e6 9 c3 ♘c5 10 ♘d4?!** *(D)*

One of White's less fortunate continuations. 10 ♗c2 is one of the better alternatives.

**10...♘xe5!**

Practically forced. 10...♘xd4? is clearly inferior: 11 cxd4 ♘xb3 12 ♕xb3 c5 13 dxc5 ♗xc5 14 ♕g3 ♕c7! 15 ♘d2! (15 ♕xg7?! 0-0-0 16 ♗f4 ♖dg8 17 ♕f6 ♗e7 18 ♕h6 ♔b8 19 ♖c1 ♕b7 is unclear) 15...0-0 16 ♘b3 ± Ivkov-Lehmann, Yugoslavia 1954.

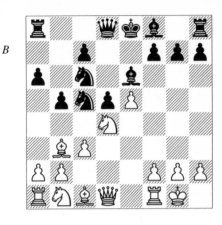

**11 f4**

Practice has shown that 11 ♕e2? ♘c4 12 ♗c2 ♕f6 13 a4 bxa4 14 ♖e1 ♗d6 15 ♕h5 g6 16 ♕h6 ♗f8 17 ♕h3 ♗e7! favours Black, as in Tal-Ree, Wijk aan Zee 1968.

**11...♘ed3! 12 f5 ♗c8 13 ♗c2**

According to the Encyclopaedia of Chess Openings (*ECO*), at this point White can try the interesting 13 ♘c6!? ♕d6 14 ♕e2+ ♔d7 15 ♘d4.

**13...♘xc1 14 ♖e1+ ♔d7!** *(D)*

This was a novelty back in 1983. With the help of this unusual king move, Black ensures the natural development of his forces, thus solving all his problems. It proves very difficult for White to find inroads to the black king, especially since his dark-squared bishop has been exchanged. Less effective is 14...♘e4?! 15 ♗xe4 dxe4 16 ♖xe4+ ♗e7 17 f6 gxf6 18 ♕xc1 ♗b7 19 ♖e2 ♕d5 with unclear play, Hatlebakk-Patterson, Ybbs U-26 Wcht 1968.

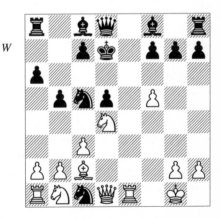

**15 a4!? ♗d6! 16 ♕xc1 ♖e8**

Exchanging pieces and preparing to transfer the king to the kingside. Black also creates the transparent threat of 17...♗xh2+.

**17 g3 ♖xe1+ 18 ♕xe1 bxa4! 19 ♕d1 ♕g5 20 ♗xa4+ ♘xa4 21 ♕xa4+ ♔e7!** (D)

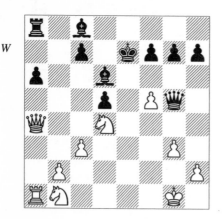

The game is practically over. The black king finds shelter without problems, while Black's material (extra pawn) and positional superiority (two bishops) proves decisive.

**22 ♕c2 ♔f8 23 b4 c5 24 bxc5 ♗xc5 25 ♔h1 ♔g8 26 ♕e2 ♗xf5**

Winning a second pawn. The game finished as follows:

**27 ♘xf5 ♕xf5 28 ♘d2 ♕c2 29 ♖f1 ♕xc3 30 ♘f3 h6 31 ♘h4 ♕e3 32 ♕h5 ♕e4+ 33 ♖f3 ♖a7 34 ♘f5 ♖b7 35 ♔g2 ♗f8 36 ♘h4 g6 37 ♘xg6 fxg6 0-1**

A very easy game, in which White was misled by *ECO*'s suggestion. Of course, the blame is all on White: all suggestions and advice others offer must be critically examined, either with the help of other chess-players or with chess software, which exists in abundance nowadays.

### Vouldis – Grivas
*Komotini 1992*

**1 e4 c5 2 ♘f3 ♘c6 3 d4 cxd4 4 ♘xd4 ♕b6 5 ♘b3 ♘f6 6 ♘c3 e6 7 ♗g5!? ♗b4! 8 ♗d3 h6 9 ♗xf6 gxf6 10 ♕f3 ♔e7!** (D)

The safest spot for the black king, supporting and being surrounded by a mass of pawns.

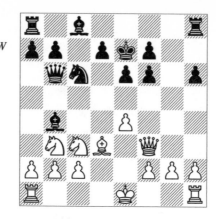

**11 0-0 a6 12 ♕g3**

A plan involving ♘d2-c4 seems preferable.

**12...♗d6! 13 ♕h4**

After 13 ♕g7 ♕d8! and ...♕g8 White will have to suffer in an inferior ending.

**13...♘e5! 14 ♔h1 ♘g6 15 ♕h5 ♘f4**

Now in order to achieve the f4-advance, White will first have to play g3, weakening the long h1-a8 diagonal which the c8-bishop will shortly occupy. In general, White faces serious problems coming up with a decent plan.

**16 ♕f3 h5! 17 ♖ae1 ♗e5**

Black's superiority increases with every move. White now resolves to free his position by exchanges.

**18 ♘e2!? ♘xe2**

18...♘g6! seems better.

**19 ♕xe2 ♕c7! 20 ♕e3 ♗f4 21 ♕h3 b5 22 ♘d4 ♗b7 23 ♘e2 ♗d6** (D)

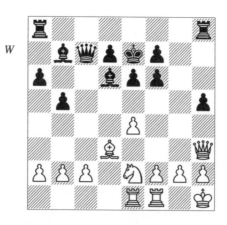

**24 a4!?**

Playing f4 would weaken rather than activate White's position. But this change of direction (from the kingside to the queenside) is further evidence that White is lacking a plan. With time-pressure approaching, White decides to complicate the position by any means instead of awaiting fate. This approach can only be commended from a practical viewpoint.

**24...bxa4! 25 ♖a1 a3! 26 bxa3 ♗c5?! 27 a4 ♗c6 28 c3 ♕a7 29 ♘f4!** *(D)*

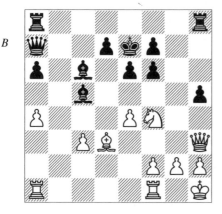

**29...h4**

29...♗xf2? would in general open lines towards the black king and, more specifically, would lead to severe problems after 30 ♕f3!.

**30 ♖ae1! ♗xa4 31 e5! fxe5 32 ♖xe5 ♗d6 33 ♖a5 ♗xf4?**

A serious mistake. Simply 33...♗c6 34 ♖xa6 ♕b7 35 ♖xa8 ♕xa8 leaves Black clearly better.

**34 ♖xa4 ♕c7 35 ♖xa6 ♖xa6 36 ♗xa6 ♗e5 37 c4 ♗f6 38 ♗b5 ♖b8 39 ♕a3+ d6 40 ♕e3 ♖a8**

Time-trouble has passed and Black retains a plus. However, the presence of opposite-coloured bishops makes the conversion of this plus to a full point rather problematic.

**41 ♕e4 ♖a2 42 h3?**

White had to play 42 g3!. The black h-pawn will prove fatal.

**42...♕b6! 43 f4 ♕d4!** *(D)*

By exchanging queens, Black increases his advantage, as he can now create a passed pawn while at the same time preventing the white king from actively participating.

**44 ♕xd4**

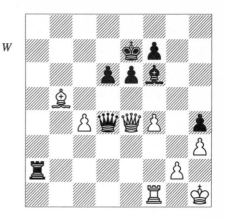

White can hardly avoid the exchange. After 44 ♕b7+ ♔f8 Black is threatening 45...♖a1 46 ♖xa1 ♕xa1+ 47 ♔h2 ♗d4!.

**44...♗xd4 45 f5**

Black was planning ...♗f2, ...f5 and ...e5-e4 – thus White's reply. In any case, Black now coasts along to victory without difficulty.

**45...♖c2! 46 fxe6 fxe6 47 ♖e1 ♗f2 48 ♖f1 ♗g3 49 ♔g1 e5 50 ♖d1 e4 51 ♔f1 ♖f2+ 52 ♔g1 ♖b2 53 ♗a6 e3 54 c5 dxc5 55 ♔f1 ♖f2+ 56 ♔g1 ♖a2 0-1**

### Vouldis – Grivas
*Rodos 1993*

**1 e4 c5 2 ♘f3 ♘c6 3 d4 cxd4 4 ♘xd4 ♕b6 5 ♘b3 ♘f6 6 ♘c3 e6 7 ♗e3 ♕c7 8 f4 ♗b4 9 ♗d3 ♗xc3+!**

Better than 9...d5 10 e5 ♘e4 11 ♗xe4 dxe4 12 0-0 ♗xc3 13 bxc3 b6 14 ♘d2 ±.

**10 bxc3 d6 11 0-0 e5** *(D)*

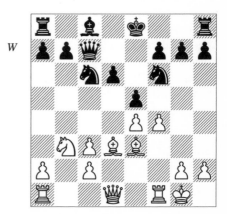

**12 ♔h1**

A theoretical novelty. 12 f5?! is popular but dubious – 12...h6! 13 ♕f3 b6 14 ♕g3 ♔f8 gives Black a very satisfactory position. Another game of the author went 12 h3 b6 13 c4 ♗b7 14 ♕e1 ♘b8 15 ♗d2 ♘bd7 16 ♖d1 0-0 17 f5 ♗a6 18 ♕e2 ♖ac8 ∓ Daifas-Grivas, Athens 1997.

**12...h6?! (D)**

In Liss-Grivas, Rishon le Zion 1993 I employed the superior 12...♘g4! 13 ♗g1 exf4 14 ♖xf4 ♘ge5 15 ♘d4 0-0 16 ♕h5 ♘g6 17 ♖f3 ♘ce5 18 ♖g3 ♘f4 19 ♕g5 ♘e6 20 ♘xe6 fxe6 21 ♗d4 b6 22 ♖b1 ♖f7, achieving a good position.

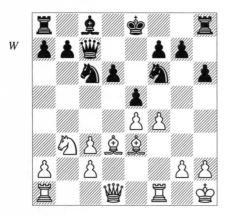

**13 ♕e1 b6 14 fxe5! dxe5 15 ♕g3 ♔f8 16 ♘d4!? ♘h5? (D)**

This move loses in spectacular style. Black should have played 16...♘e7! 17 ♘f3 (17 ♘f5? ♘xf5 18 exf5 ♕xc3) 17...♘g6 18 ♘h4! ♘xh4 19 ♕xh4 ♘e8! with unclear play (but not 19...♘g4? 20 ♗c4!! with advantage, 19...♕e7? 20 ♗g5! or 19...♕c6 20 a4 ♗b7 21 ♖f5).

**17 ♕g6!! exd4 18 cxd4 ♘f6 19 ♖xf6!**

Having sacrificed a piece, White offers a further exchange, eventually getting through to the black king.

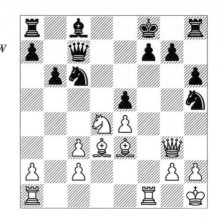

**19...gxf6 20 ♕xf6 ♖g8**

20...♔g8 21 ♖f1! ♕e7 22 ♕xc6 ♗b7 23 ♕c4 ♖c8 24 ♕b3, intending d5 and ♗d4, is also winning for White, but perhaps Black should have tried this instead of the text-move.

**21 ♗f4!**

This move had escaped Black's attention, but the black king surely won't escape White's!

**21...♕d7 22 ♗d6+ ♔e8 (D)**

Or 22...♘e7 23 ♗c4 ♖g7 24 ♖f1!.

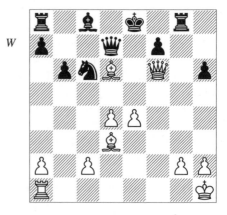

**23 ♗b5 ♗b7 24 d5 ♖c8**

24...♕d8 25 dxc6! ♕xf6 26 c7+.

**25 ♖d1 a6 26 dxc6 ♗xc6 27 ♖d5! 1-0**

# Attacking the King: Castling on the Same Side

In the present chapter, the second revolving around an attack on the king, we shall examine cases where both players have castled on the same side, i.e. they have – theoretically speaking – safeguarded their king.

The evaluation of one's potential for an attack against the king will play a significant role in this case. When the opponent's king is stuck in the centre or when the two players have castled on opposite sides, things are somewhat easier, at least where evaluation and calculation are concerned.

In the present case however, things are hardly clear since, in order to succeed in an attack, we often have to neglect the safety of our own king – though this is not always the case.

First of all we have to mention that the set of rules, requirements and conditions mentioned in the previous chapter also applies, almost in its entirety, to this chapter as well. However, the relative importance of these guidelines changes somewhat. More specifically, the most significant elements in this particular case are:

1) Space advantage, in general, and more specifically on the flank on which we intend to attack.

2) Ability to transfer forces to the flank on which we will attack.

3) Material superiority in that flank.

4) Presence of pawns and/or targets in the opposing king's defensive cover.

5) Absence (permanent or temporary) of the opponent's defensive forces.

Naturally, an attack of any kind does not necessarily aim at checkmating the king; it can also lead to significant material or positional gains.

The defending side must organize its defence always keeping in mind the possibility of counterattacking. The weaknesses possibly created

by the opponent during the prosecution of the attack can serve as targets. Moreover, the player on the receiving end of the attack often seeks activity on the other flank or the centre. This leads to very interesting games, where the winner is determined by the correct realization of each side's plans.

To quote one fundamental principle of chess: "a weakness is a liability (positional or tactical) that can be attacked; otherwise it is not considered a weakness". Consequently, if we are compelled to move the pawns protecting our king we have to judge whether this makes our king accessible to the opponent's forces and to what extent. This will help us determine whether by acting so we are really creating a weakness. The reader should note that while there are be rules and generalities, there will always be exceptions, and in chess the specific considerations will always trump the general ones.

**Hebden – Grivas**
*Iraklion 1984*

**1 e4 e5 2 f4 d5 3 exd5 c6**

White has opened the game with clearly aggressive intentions by playing the King's Gambit. Black does not evade the challenge, offering a countergambit of his own.

**4 ♘c3**

One should beware of the typical error 4 fxe5?? ♕h4+ 5 ♔e2 ♕e4+ 6 ♔f2 ♗c5+ 7 d4 ♗xd4+ 8 ♔g3 ♗xe5+ 9 ♔f2 ♗d4+ 10 ♔g3 ♕g6+ 11 ♔f4 ♕f5+ 12 ♔g3 ♗f2# (0-1) Perenyi-Grivas, Athens 1984.

**4...exf4 5 ♘f3 ♗d6 6 d4 ♘e7 7 dxc6 ♘bxc6 8 d5 ♘b4 9 ♗c4** *(D)*

**9...♗f5!?**

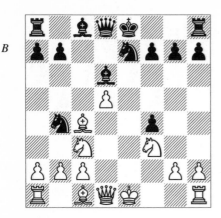

B

This move was suggested by Henley after he tried 9...0-0 in Hebden-Henley, New York 1983, which proved slightly better for White.

**10 ♗b3! 0-0 11 0-0**

White's plan is to play a3, ♘d4 and then capture the f4-pawn. Black must tread carefully.

**11...♗g4! 12 ♘e4 ♘f5 13 c3! ♘a6 14 ♗c2 ♘h4?!**

An initial inaccuracy. 14...♘c5! is correct. After 15 ♘xd6 ♕xd6 16 c4 (16 ♗xf5 ♗xf5 17 ♘d4 ♗e4 is unclear) 16...♘h4! 17 ♗xh7+ ♔h8! Black has compensation for the pawn in a complex position that offers plenty of possibilities to both sides.

**15 ♘xd6 ♗xf3?** *(D)*

Black definitely had to play 15...♕xd6 16 ♗xh7+ ♔h8 17 ♗c2 ♖ae8! with unclear consequences. Now his king turns out to be very exposed.

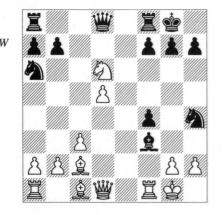

W

**16 ♕d3! f5**

16...g6 17 ♗xf4 ♗xg2 18 ♖f2! is also losing for Black.

**17 ♗xf4**

White's superiority is obvious. His pieces cooperate well and his initiative is irresistible.

**17...♗xg2 18 ♖f2 ♘g6 19 ♘xf5! ♗xd5 20 ♖e1! ♗f7 21 ♗d6 ♕b6 22 ♗xf8 ♖xf8 23 ♖e3! 1-0**

Black resigned due to 23...♘c5 24 ♘e7+ ♔h8 25 ♕xg6!!.

## Grivas – Skembris
*Athens 1984*

**1 d4 ♘f6 2 c4 e6 3 ♘c3 ♗b4 4 ♗g5 h6 5 ♗h4 c5** *(D)*

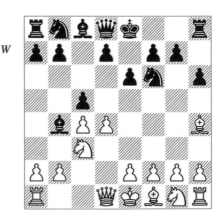

W

**6 d5**

The only move promising White any advantage. 6 ♖c1 cxd4 7 ♕xd4 ♘c6 8 ♗xf6 ♘xd4 9 ♗xd8 ♔xd8 10 e3 ♘c6 11 a3 ♗e7 (11...♗xc3+ 12 ♖xc3 b6 13 ♘f3 ♗b7 14 ♗e2 ♔e7 = Grivas-Dawson, Oakham 1984) 12 ♘f3 f5!? 13 ♗e2 ♗f6 14 0-0 ♔e7 15 ♖fd1 b6 16 b4 ♖d8 17 ♘d4 ♗b7 18 ♗f3 ♖ab8 = Grivas-Leko, Iraklion ECC 1997.

**6...♗xc3+ 7 bxc3 e5 8 ♕c2**

8 d6!? is an interesting move.

**8...d6 9 ♘f3 ♘bd7 10 e3**

10 e4 is also often played, but with entirely different ideas from the text-move.

**10...♕e7 11 ♘d2**

The battle revolves around the e4-square. The side that gains control of this square will be able to claim the advantage.

**11...g5 12 ♗g3** *(D)*

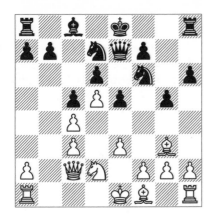

**12...♘h5?!**

Inaccurate. 12...e4! is much better: 13 h4 (13 0-0-0!? can also be considered, as in Spassky-Kholmov, Moscow 1957) 13...♖g8 14 ♗e2 ♘b6 with unclear play.

**13 ♗e2!**

13 ♗d3?! ♘f4! would be a bad idea for White.

**13...♘df6**

13...♘xg3?! 14 fxg3! or 13...♘f4?! 14 exf4 exf4 15 ♗xf4 gxf4 16 0-0! would be clearly inferior. Black must keep the position (and the f-file in particular) closed.

**14 0-0 0-0 15 ♖ae1**

Preparing to push f4. Black has lost the fight for the e4-square and has problems coming up with an active plan.

**15...♔g7 16 ♗d3**

After the careless 16 f4?! exf4 17 exf4 ♘xg3! 18 hxg3 ♕e3+ 19 ♔h2 ♖e8 Black would be fine.

**16...♗d7** *(D)*

**17 h3!?**

Planning ♗h2, g4 and f4. Once again, 17 f4?! is premature, due to 17...♘xg3 18 hxg3 ♘h5.

**17...♘g8**

17...♘xg3?! would now be erroneous, in view of 18 fxg3 g4 19 ♗f5!. Black should probably have preferred 17...♖ae8 18 ♗h2 ♔h8 ±.

**18 ♗f5!**

Black was threatening 18...f5!.

**18...♔h8! 19 ♗g4!**

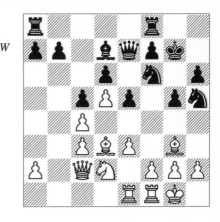

Again practically forced, to meet the threat of 19...♗xf5 20 ♕xf5 ♘g7 21 ♕c2 f5.

**19...♘g7?**

Black should have consented to a slightly worse ending after 19...♗xg4 20 hxg4 ♘xg3 21 fxg3 ♕d7 22 ♕f5. White will place his knight on e4 and then play on the queenside with ♖b1 and a4-a5, securing some advantage. After the text-move, White has the opportunity to open up the kingside and whip up a menacing attack against the black king.

**20 ♗xd7 ♕xd7 21 f4!** *(D)*

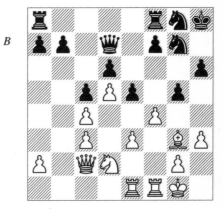

Finally!

**21...exf4**

Forced, as 21...f6 22 fxe5 dxe5 (22...fxe5 23 ♕g6!) is definitely not to Black's liking.

**22 exf4 f5**

Other moves do not diminish White's advantage: 22...g4 23 f5! or 22...♘f5 23 ♗h2 ♖ae8 24 ♘e4.

**23 fxg5 hxg5 24 ♘f3 ♕d8 25 h4!**

Opening more lines – the black king is already feeling the heat.

**25...gxh4**

If 25...g4 then 26 ♘g5!.

**26 ♗xh4!**

It is important to control the g5-square: not 26 ♘xh4?! ♕g5!.

**26...♕d7 27 ♗g5! ♖ae8 28 ♕f2! ♕f7 29 ♗f4! ♖d8** *(D)*

29...♕f6 30 ♕g3! is also inadequate for Black.

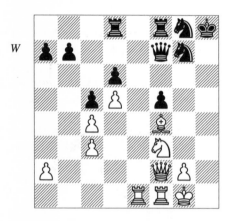

White has succeeded in destroying the black king's cover and bringing his pieces over to the kingside, where the battle will be decided. His position is strategically won, which implies that several tactical shots are lurking around. All he has to do is spot them!

**30 ♘g5! ♕g6**

Black is defenceless after 30...♕h5 31 ♖e3! and 32 ♖h3.

**31 ♕h4+! ♕h5 32 ♕xh5+ ♘xh5 33 ♘e6**

White's positional superiority has been transformed into a material advantage. The black king has survived, but only after surrendering material. White exploited his extra exchange as follows:

**33...♖a8 34 ♘xf8 ♘xf4 35 ♖xf4 ♖xf8 36 ♖e6 ♖f6 37 ♖xf6 ♘xf6 38 ♖xf5 ♔g7 39 ♖f3 ♘e4 40 ♖e3 ♘d2 41 ♖e7+ ♔f6 42 ♖xb7 a5 43 ♖b8 ♘xc4 44 ♖e8 ♔f5 45 ♖e6 a4 46 ♔f2 a3 47 ♔e2 ♘b6 48 ♖xd6 ♘a4 49 ♔d2 ♔e5 50 ♖a6 ♘b2 51 d6 ♘c4+ 52 ♔d3 ♘xd6 53 ♖xd6**
**1-0**

## Grivas – Stipić
*Bela Crkva 1987*

**1 d4 ♘f6 2 c4 g6 3 ♘c3 ♗g7 4 e4 d6 5 f4 c5 6 d5 0-0 7 ♘f3 e6 8 ♗e2 exd5 9 cxd5 ♘a6 10 e5 ♘e8 11 0-0 ♗g4?!** *(D)*

An unsuccessful novelty. The theoretical continuation is 11...♘ac7 with White enjoying the better chances.

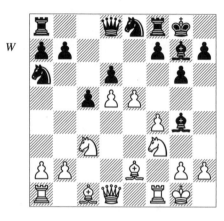

**12 ♘g5! ♗xe2 13 ♕xe2 ♘ac7 14 ♗e3!**

The only good move, completing White's development and supporting his central initiative. The direct 14 e6? fxe6 15 ♘xe6 ♘xe6 16 dxe6 ♕e7 17 ♗d2 ♘c7 would leave Black better, while 14 ♕f3? h6! is totally useless.

**14...b6 15 ♖ad1**

All the white pieces are actively placed and support White's space advantage and central control, as well as a dangerous initiative. A combination of these elements will usually suffice to bring victory.

**15...dxe5**

Black accepts the challenge as 15...♕e7 16 ♘f3 dxe5 17 fxe5 ♗xe5? 18 ♗h6 is hopeless.

**16 d6!** *(D)*

**16...♘e6**

The alternative was 16...♘xd6 17 ♘ge4 ♘ce8 18 ♘b5! ♕e7 (18...♘xe4 19 ♖xd8 ♖xd8 20 fxe5) 19 ♘bxd6 ♘xd6 20 ♘xd6 exf4 21 ♖xf4 ♗e5 22 ♖e4 f5 23 ♗g5! with a significant advantage for White.

**17 ♘xe6 fxe6 18 fxe5 ♗xe5**

White's task would have been more complicated after 18...♖xf1+ 19 ♖xf1 ♗xe5 20 ♗h6

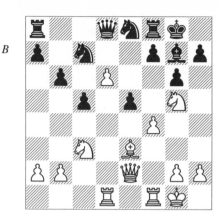

B

&xd6 (20...&xh2+ 21 &xh2 ♕h4+ 22 &g1
♕xh6 23 ♕xe6+ &h8 24 d7!) 21 ♕xe6+ &h8
22 ♘e4, but with the same positive result for
White.

**19 ♖xf8+ &xf8 20 &h6+ &g7 21 ♖f1+
&g8**

21...♘f6 22 &xg7+ &xg7 23 ♕e5 is also
losing for Black.

**22 ♕xe6+ &h8** (D)

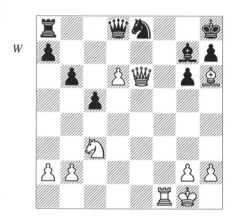

W

White's advantage is crystal clear, but it is of
a purely dynamic nature. Consequently, it needs
to be transformed to material gain or some
other kind of stable advantage. The black pieces
are totally uncoordinated and restricted to their
back two ranks, while the unfortunate placement
of the e8-knight cuts Black's camp in two. As a
result, Black's defensive capability is greatly
hampered. It should come as no surprise that
White has a decisive tactical shot that immediately converts his great advantage into victory.

**23 ♕e5!!**

With the threat of 24 ♖f8#.

**23...&g8**

There is no better answer: 23...♘xd6 24
♕xg7# or 23...♕xd6 24 &xg7+.

**24 ♘d5! 1-0**

White threatens 25 ♘e7+ &h8 26 ♖f8#, and
there is no satisfactory defence: 24...♕xd6
(24...&xe5 25 ♖f8#; 24...&xh6 25 ♘e7+) 25
♘e7+ &h8 26 ♖f8#. An unusual position,
where Black can choose to capture one of three
white pieces, but none of these moves will ensure his survival!

## Makropoulos – Grivas
*Athens 1989*

**1 e4 c5 2 ♘f3 e6 3 d3 d5 4 ♘bd2 ♘c6 5 g3
&d6** (D)

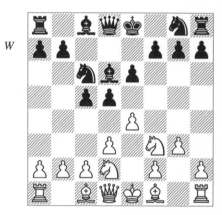

W

One of the best ways to meet White's King's
Indian Attack set-up, in my opinion.

**6 &g2 ♘ge7 7 0-0 0-0 8 ♖e1 &c7 9 c3
♖b8!?**

A new move. A satisfactory alternative is
9...a5 10 a4 b6 11 exd5 exd5 12 d4 with chances
for both sides.

**10 a3**

10 ♘b3!? b6 11 exd5 exd5 12 d4 is another
possible plan.

**10...a5 11 a4?!**

White fails to meet the demands of the position. He should have continued with 11 ♖b1
and b4, pursuing activity on the queenside.

**11...b6 12 ♕c2 &a6 13 &f1 ♕d7!**

Black has completed his development in a satisfactory way and now prepares to develop his initiative on the kingside with the help of ...f5. White is still floundering, unable to find a way to meet Black's actions.

**14 ♘b1 ♘g6 15 ♘a3** *(D)*

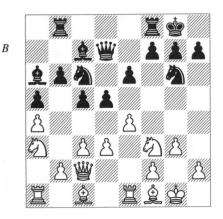

**15...f5!**

The inaccurate 15...♘ge5?! 16 ♘d2! (but not 16 ♘xe5? ♘xe5 17 ♔g2 c4! with advantage) would present White with fewer problems.

**16 exf5 exf5**

Black could also continue with 16...♖xf5 17 ♗h3 ♘ce5! 18 ♘xe5 ♘xe5 19 ♗xf5 ♘f3+ 20 ♔f1 ♘xe1 21 ♗xh7+ ♔xh7 22 ♔xe1 e5!, obtaining excellent compensation for his minimal material investment (one pawn).

**17 ♗h3?**

This is a serious mistake. The same would apply to 17 ♘b5? ♗xb5 18 axb5 ♘ce5 19 ♘xe5 ♘xe5 20 ♗g2 c4! (or 20...f4!? 21 ♗xf4 ♖xf4! 22 gxf4 ♘g6 with an attack) 21 dxc4 dxc4 ∓. White should have preferred 17 ♗g2 f4, although Black retains the initiative.

**17...♘ce5! 18 ♘xe5 ♘xe5 19 ♖d1 d4!**

Opening up the h1-a8 diagonal. Black's attack is gaining in strength.

**20 ♗g2 ♗b7! 21 cxd4** *(D)*

It is hard to come up with good advice for White. After 21 f4 ♘f3+! 22 ♔h1 g5! 23 fxg5 (23 ♖f1 g4 intending ...h5-h4) 23...f4 Black also has a strong attack.

**21...♘f3+! 22 ♔h1 ♘xd4 23 ♕c4+ ♔h8 24 ♖g1**

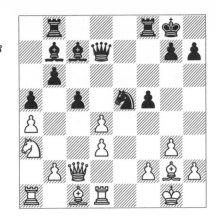

Forced, due to the threat of 24...♗xg2+ 25 ♔xg2 ♕c6+.

**24...♘f3! 25 ♘b5**

White gives up an exchange, hoping to slow down Black's attack. Naturally, this sacrifice turns out to be inadequate, but White can hardly be blamed for his choice. 25 ♖d1 f4 26 ♗xf4 ♗xf4 27 gxf4 ♗d5 28 ♕b5 ♕g4 is disastrous for him.

**25...♘xg1 26 ♘xc7 ♗xg2+ 27 ♔xg2 ♕xc7 28 ♗f4 ♕b7+ 29 ♔xg1 ♖be8**

Black has a winning position and the rest is just a matter of technique.

**30 d4 cxd4 31 ♕xd4 ♖e4 32 ♕d6 ♖fe8 33 ♗e3 ♖4e6 34 ♕d1 ♕e4 35 ♖a3 ♖g6 36 ♖d3 h6 37 ♖d4 ♕e6 38 h3** *(D)*

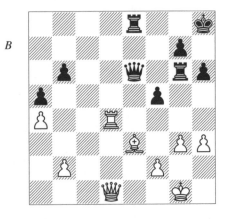

**38...♖xg3+!**

*Simplification of the position and transition to a winning endgame is the approved method in positions with extra material.*

**39 fxg3 ♕xe3+ 40 ♔g2 ♕e2+! 41 ♕xe2**

Nothing would change after 41 ♔g1 ♕xd1+ 42 ♖xd1 ♖e3! 43 ♔f2 ♖b3 44 ♖d2 ♖b4.

**41...♖xe2+ 42 ♔f3 ♖xb2 43 ♖d6 ♖b4! 44 h4 ♔h7 45 h5 ♖xa4! 46 ♖xb6 ♖g4 47 ♖b5** *(D)*

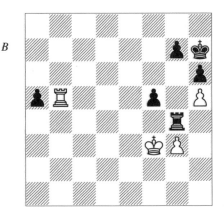

**47...a4! 48 ♖a5**

White also loses after 48 ♖xf5 ♖g5! 49 ♖f8 ♖a5! 50 ♖b8 a3 51 ♖b1 ♖xh5.

**48...♔g8 49 ♖a7 ♔f8 50 ♔f2 f4 51 gxf4 ♖xf4+ 52 ♔g3 ♖b4 53 ♔h3 ♔g8 54 ♔g3 ♔h7 55 ♔h3 ♖b3+ 56 ♔g4 ♖a3 57 ♖a8 ♖a1 58 ♔g3 a3 59 ♔h2 a2 60 ♔g2 ♖b1 0-1**

White resigned in view of 61 ♖xa2 ♖b5 and 62...♖xh5.

## Gelfand – Grivas

*European Team Ch, Haifa 1989*

**1 d4 ♘f6 2 c4 g6 3 ♘c3 ♗g7 4 e4 d6 5 ♗e2 0-0 6 ♘f3 e5 7 0-0 ♘c6 8 d5 ♘e7 9 ♗g5!?** *(D)*

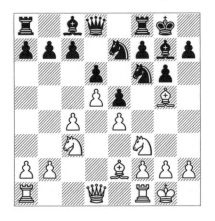

One of White's many possibilities in this position, although admittedly it is not very popular.

**9...♘d7?!**

I believe this is unsatisfactory. Theory suggests 9...h6! 10 ♗xf6 ♗xf6, intending ...♔g7, ...♘g8 and ...♗e7. 9...h5?! is also not ideal for Black: 10 g3 f6 11 ♗d2 f5 12 exf5 ♘xf5 13 ♘e4! ± Ftačnik-Kr.Georgiev, Palma de Mallorca 1989.

**10 ♘d2 f5 11 exf5?!**

White should play 11 f3 ±.

**11...gxf5 12 f4 ♘f6**

12...e4?! is not good in view of 13 ♘b3! intending ♘d4-e6.

**13 ♗h5?**

An incomprehensible move and, at the same time, a serious mistake. 13 fxe5 dxe5 14 c5 with unclear play should have been preferred.

**13...e4!**

13...♘g6?! would only justify White's last move: 14 ♗xg6 hxg6 15 ♘f3 e4 16 ♘h4.

**14 ♘b3 c5! 15 dxc6**

In a practical sense the only move, as otherwise White would be deprived of active play. But this exchange weakens White's central influence.

**15...bxc6 16 ♔h1 d5** *(D)*

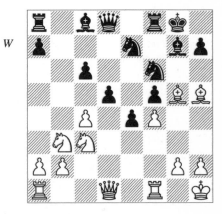

**17 ♗e2**

Admitting the mistake mentioned earlier. 17 cxd5?! ♘exd5! 18 ♘xd5 ♕xd5 would be good for Black.

**17...♔h8!**

Black has been planning to sacrifice an exchange with ...♖b8xb3 so as to dominate the centre, but White has prepared an antidote: 17...Rb8? 18 cxd5 Nexd5 19 Bc4!. Now, however, this threat is really dangerous and White decides to rule it out.

**18 Bh4!? Ng6! 19 Bf2**

Other moves are unsatisfactory: 19 Bxf6 Bxf6 20 cxd5 cxd5 21 Nxd5 Bxb2 or 19 Be1 Rb8! 20 Nd4 Wd6! – Black is better in both cases.

**19...Nxf4!**

Strong and at the same time forced, in view of the positional threat of 20 Bd4.

**20 Bc5 Nxe2 21 Bxf8** *(D)*

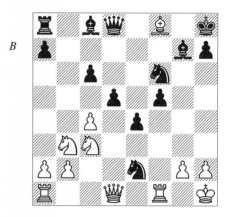

**21...Ng3+!**

An important *zwischenzug*, weakening the white king's shield. Black's compensation is multi-faceted: strong centre, two bishops, good piece coordination. All these factors contribute to a strong attack against the white king.

**22 hxg3 Wxf8 23 cxd5 cxd5!**

23...Ng4? is a serious mistake: 24 Wxg4! fxg4 25 Rxf8+ Bxf8 26 dxc6.

**24 Nxd5 Ng4! 25 Wd2?!**

White should have tried to bail out into an inferior endgame with 25 Wxg4 fxg4 26 Rxf8+ Bxf8 27 Nf6 Bg7 28 Nxe4 Bxb2. In practice though, it is hard to make such a decision – especially if you are a much stronger player than your opponent.

**25...Ba6! 26 Wg5**

White is forced to return material. 26 Rfd1 is met by 26...Be5 and ...e3, and 26 Rfc1 by 26...Rd8!.

**26...Bxf1 27 Rxf1 e3!**

Solving the problem of the f5-pawn's defence in the best possible manner.

**28 Nc1** *(D)*

Or: 28 Rxf5 e2! 29 Rxf8+ Rxf8; 28 Nxe3 Bh6 29 Wxf5 Nxe3 30 We5+ Wg7.

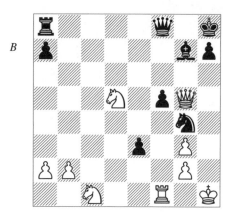

Black is obviously better in this position, not only due to his dangerous attacking potential but also his well-placed pieces. In addition, the passed e3-pawn is very dangerous, while the black bishop is clearly superior to the white knights.

**28...Bh6?**

The tactical sequence 28...Wc5! 29 Nc3 (29 Ne7 Wc4! 30 Re1 Bf6) 29...Wc4! 30 Rxf5 Bxc3 31 bxc3 Rg8! (31...e2? 32 We7!) 32 We7 Wxc3 33 Rf1 We5! 34 Wxe5+ Nxe5 would secure Black a sizeable advantage but, being in severe time-pressure, he could not calculate this line properly. The following moves were flashed out by both sides.

**29 Wh4 Re8 30 Ne2 Re4 31 Kg1 Nf2 32 Wf6+! Wxf6 33 Nxf6 Rc4 34 Rc1 Rxc1+ 35 Nxc1 Bg7 36 Nd5 Bxb2 37 Nxe3 Ne4?**

Black misses his last chance. After 37...Ng4! 38 Nxg4 fxg4 an ending arises that is very favourable for Black (bishop vs knight in an open position and better structure).

**38 Ne2 Nd6 39 Kf2 Kg7 40 Kf3 Kf6 ½-½**

**Lukacs – Grivas**
*Budapest 1993*

**1 d4 Nf6 2 c4 g6 3 Nc3 Bg7 4 e4 d6 5 Nf3 0-0 6 Be2 e5 7 0-0 Nc6 8 d5 Ne7 9 Ne1 Nd7 10**

♘d3 f5 11 ♗d2 ♞f6 12 f3 f4 13 g4 g5 14 ♗e1 h5 15 h3 ♞g6 16 ♔g2 ♖f7 *(D)*

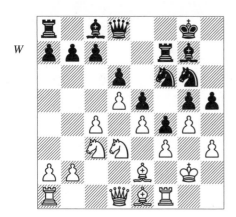

**17 ♗f2!?**

After a heavily theoretical opening White deviates from theory with this move. In previous games 17 c5?! had been tried, but with unsatisfactory results. Both sides' aims are clear: White will play on the queenside and Black on the kingside.

**17...♗f8 18 b4 ♖h7 19 ♖h1 ♗e7!**

Black wishes to clear his back rank so as to facilitate the transfer of his major pieces to the kingside.

**20 ♕b3 ♔g7 21 c5 ♗d7!**

Black organizes his defence. 21...♕h8?! would be premature due to 22 ♞b5!.

**22 ♖ac1 a6! 23 a4 hxg4 24 hxg4 ♞h4+ 25 ♗xh4 ♖xh4! 26 ♖xh4**

Nothing better for White is apparent, as after 26 b5 axb5 27 axb5 ♕g8! 28 b6 c6! Black can feel happy.

**26...gxh4 27 ♕c4!?** *(D)*

And not the mistaken 27 cxd6? h3+! 28 ♔h1 cxd6 29 a5 b6! with a clear advantage for Black.

**27...h3+! 28 ♔h1**

28 ♔xh3?? ♕h8+ 29 ♔g2 ♕h4.

**28...♕h8 29 c6! bxc6 30 dxc6 ♗c8 31 ♖g1 ♞h7 32 ♕b3?!**

The immediate 32 ♞d5 ♗e6 is preferable.

**32...♞g5 33 ♞d5 ♗e6 34 b5?**

Opening up the position does not help White's cause at all, as the weaknesses on the dark squares now come to the fore. White should instead have stayed put with 34 ♗d1.

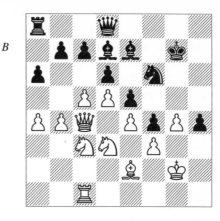

**34...axb5 35 axb5 ♗xd5! 36 ♕xd5 ♕b8!**

Black is about to invade on the dark squares (...♕b6-f2/e3), pursuing his attack against the white king. This sudden change of direction is rather unusual, but quite logical and very effective.

**37 ♞xe5!?** *(D)*

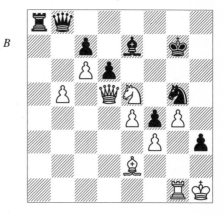

Seeking salvation in irrational complications.

**37...dxe5?!**

Black did not have to oblige. In fact, his position was so good that the simple and consistent 37...♕b6! would have won: 38 ♞c4 (38 ♞d3 ♕e3!) 38...♕f2 39 ♕d1 (39 ♕d3 ♖a1 40 ♗d1 ♖a2!) 39...♖a2 40 ♞d2 ♕e3 –+.

**38 ♕xe5+ ♗f6 39 ♕xf4 ♖a2?**

A serious mistake in time-trouble. 39...♕b6! is a simple win.

**40 e5?**

White returns the favour for the same reasons. 40 ♗c4? ♖f2 41 ♖f1 ♕b6 is just as bad as the game continuation, but he could have saved the draw by 40 ♖d1!! ♖xe2 (40...♘f7? 41 ♗c4! or 40...♕f8? 41 ♕xc7+ ♔g6 42 ♕h2 ±) 41 ♖d7+ ♘f7 42 g5 ♖e1+ and perpetual check.

**40...♗e7 41 ♕c4 ♖b2!**

The only way to win! Instead, 41...♖d2? 42 f4 ♕b6 43 fxg5 ♕f2 (43...♕e3? loses to 44 ♖f1!) 44 ♕e6! leads to a likely draw.

**42 f4 ♖b4! 43 ♕c1 ♘e4 44 f5** *(D)*

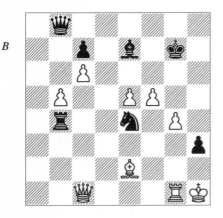

**44...♕d8!!**

Black returns the extra piece in order to dominate the position by destroying White's only source of counterplay, his pawn-mass on the kingside. In this way Black also opens further lines towards the white king. The remaining black pieces cooperate to their full extent and create decisive threats.

**45 f6+ ♗xf6 46 exf6+ ♕xf6**

Now the immediate threat is 47...♘f2+ 48 ♔h2 ♕e5+ 49 ♖g3 ♘e4.

**47 ♕e3 ♕e5! 0-1**

White has no defence: 48 ♕f3 (48 ♖f1 ♘g3+; 48 g5 ♖b3!; 48 ♗d3 ♖b2!) 48...♖b2 49 ♕f5 ♘f2+!! 50 ♕xf2 ♖xe2 51 ♕g3 ♘e4+.

## Grivas – Velikov
*Xanthi 1991*

**1 ♘f3 d5 2 c4 dxc4 3 e3 ♘f6 4 ♗xc4 e6 5 0-0 a6?!**

Pointless. The immediate 5...c5 is preferable.

**6 b3 c5 7 ♗b2** *(D)*

**7...♘c6**

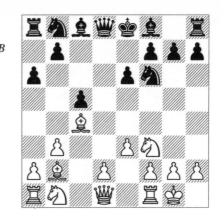

The standard 7...b5?! is less attractive here due to 8 ♗e2 ♗b7 9 a4!.

**8 ♗e2 ♗e7 9 d3 0-0 10 ♘bd2 b6 11 a3 ♗b7 12 ♕c2 ♖c8 13 ♖ac1 ♘d5 14 ♖fd1 ♗d6**

Black is somewhat lacking in space and should have instead considered exchanges, which would ease his cramp. A logical course is 14...♗f6 15 ♘e4 ♗xb2 16 ♕xb2 ±.

**15 ♗f1 ♗b8 16 ♘c4 ♘de7 17 ♕e2!**

Intending 18 d4! with the initiative.

**17...♘f5 18 g3 b5?!**

18...f6!?, intending ...e5, is better. Now the c5-pawn becomes particularly weak.

**19 ♘cd2 ♕b6 20 ♗g2 ♖fd8** *(D)*

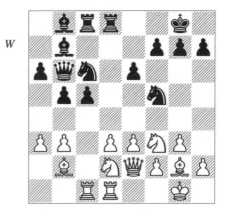

**21 ♖c2!**

Preparing to exert pressure on the weak c5-pawn. Naturally, this is not White's real target, as it can be defended rather easily. White's idea lies in luring Black's pieces away from the kingside, and then to become active on that flank.

**21...♘ce7 22 ♖dc1 ♘g6 23 e4! ♘fe7**

After 23...♘d4 24 ♘xd4 cxd4 25 b4! followed by ♘b3 and ♗h3 White will dominate.

**24 h4!**

The attack starts rolling!

**24...♘f8 25 h5 h6 26 ♘h2 ♕d6 (D)**

Or 26...e5 27 ♘g4 f6 28 ♘e3!.

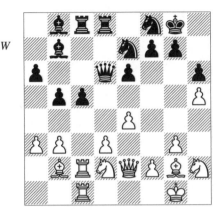

White has managed to activate all his pieces, in sharp contrast to Black, whose pieces are still searching for greener pastures, away from the kingside. This is the signal for White to commence the main attack, which proves extremely dangerous.

**27 ♘g4! ♕xd3 28 ♘xh6+! gxh6**

28...♔h7 29 ♕g4! is of no help to Black.

**29 ♕g4+ ♘eg6 30 hxg6 ♘xg6 31 ♗f6! ♔h7 32 ♘f3! (D)**

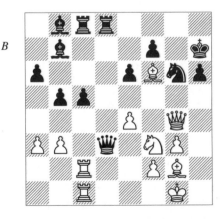

The white pieces flow towards the black king with minimum effort. The threat now is

♕h5 followed by ♘g5+ and Black cannot defend adequately against this.

**32...♗d6 33 ♖d2 ♕xb3 34 ♕h5 ♗f8 35 ♖xd8 ♖xd8 36 ♗xd8 c4 37 ♗f6 ♕xa3 38 ♖d1 ♗c6**

Or 38...c3 39 ♖d8 c2 40 ♘g5+ ♔g8 41 ♕xh6 c1♕+ 42 ♔h2 ♕xg5 43 ♕g7#.

**39 ♖d8 c3 40 ♘g5+ 1-0**

## Grivas – G. Georgadze
*Dortmund 1990*

**1 d4 d5 2 c4 e6 3 ♘c3 ♗b4 4 e3 ♘f6 5 a3 ♗xc3+ 6 bxc3 0-0 7 cxd5 exd5 8 ♗d3 b6?!**

8...c5 is more common.

**9 ♘e2 ♗a6 (D)**

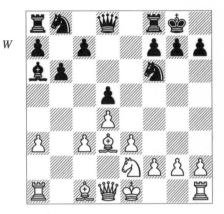

**10 0-0**

Another good option is 10 ♗xa6 ♘xa6 11 ♕d3 ♕c8 12 0-0 c5 13 f3 ± Szabo-Smyslov, Budapest 1949. On the other hand, 10 ♗b1?! ♘e4! 11 ♗b2 ♕g5 allows Black to seize the initiative.

**10...♕c8 11 ♗b1!?**

Seen less often than 11 ♗c2 or 11 f3.

**11...c5 12 f3**

The entire game revolves around the e4-square. If White achieves the e4 advance under favourable circumstances he will obtain the advantage; otherwise it will pass to Black, who will be able to exploit his queenside pawn-majority.

**12...♘c6 13 ♖e1 ♖e8 14 ♘g3**

14 g4!? followed by ♘g3 and ♖a2-g2 is an interesting suggestion by Skembris.

**14...♕d7** *(D)*

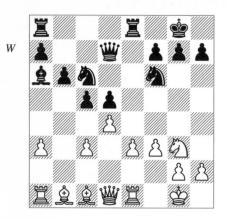

Black tries to prevent the e4 advance in an indirect way, applying pressure on the d4-pawn. This strategy is very common and quite effective.

**15 a4! ♗c4 16 ♗a3**

16 dxc5 bxc5 17 ♗a3 d4! would be quite unclear.

**16...cxd4 17 cxd4 g6 18 ♗b2! ♖ad8 19 ♗c3!**

White prevents a possible ...♘a5 and initiates a pretty regrouping of White's pieces, finally getting ready for the e4-advance.

**19...a6**

Black proceeds with his only active plan, the mobilization of his queenside majority.

**20 ♗c2 b5 21 ♕d2 ♕d6 22 axb5 axb5 23 ♖ad1 b4 24 ♗b2 b3 25 ♗b1**

White is finally all set for the long-awaited central advance, which will allow him to attack in the centre and on the kingside. Black's only sensible reaction is to put pressure on the b2-bishop, which blockades Black's passed pawn.

**25...♘d7! 26 e4 ♘b6**

Opening up the centre with 26...dxe4 would only benefit White, who is better prepared for such play.

**27 e5! ♕f8** *(D)*

White's superiority is obvious due to his attacking chances. Naturally, if the game reached an ending White would be lost but we are still in the middlegame!

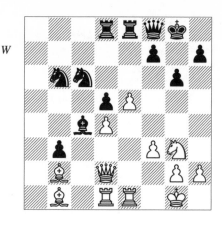

**28 f4?**

White should have catered for the b2-bishop as well! The optimal solution lay in 28 ♕c1!! ♖a8 (28...♘a4? 29 ♗a3 ♕g7 {29...b2 30 ♗xb2 ♖b8 31 ♗a1} 30 ♘e4! ±) 29 h4! ♘b4 30 ♗a3 ♖a7!? 31 h5 ♖ea8 32 ♗xb4 ♕xb4 33 e6! with a very strong, probably decisive, attack.

**28...f5! 29 exf6?**

Completely losing control of the position. Again 29 ♕c1 was better, intending h4-h5 and a future sacrifice on f5.

**29...♕xf6 30 f5 ♘a4 31 ♗a1 ♔g7!** *(D)*

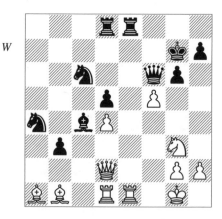

White's position is now lost, since his pieces have lost their functionality and especially the a1-bishop looks pathetic.

**32 fxg6 hxg6 33 ♘f1 ♖xe1 34 ♖xe1 ♖b8 35 ♕d1 ♖f8 36 ♘g3 b2 37 ♗xb2 ♘xb2 38 ♕c1 ♘xd4 39 h3 ♕f2+ 0-1**

# Attacking the King: Castling on Opposite Sides

This chapter, completing our coverage of the types of attack against the opponent's king, covers the most common case in practice. Positions with castling on opposite sides regularly arise from several openings and a lot of examples can be found in openings such as the Sicilian and the King's Indian.

First of all, we must bear in mind that the guidelines stated in previous chapters generally apply in this case as well, with very few exceptions.

There is, however, a very significant element in the case we shall examine now, namely the brutality and 'necessity for success' of attacks on opposite flanks. In the previous chapter, a possible failure of the attack to attain its target was not necessarily disastrous, as long as no serious weaknesses had been created in the process. In the case of castling on opposite sides however, a possible failure will usually imply easy success for our opponent. In this chapter we are not only hunters, but also possible prey!

Practice has shown that a significant percentage of games featuring mutual attacks on opposite flanks are decided by one tempo. One inaccurate move, one lost tempo, one mistaken calculation – all these are immediately exploitable by our opponent.

In view of the above, deep opening preparation, accurate judgement and good calculating skills are essential prerequisites for success. Of course, there will always be exceptions. *The only absolute rule is that there are no absolute rules!*

## Kotronias – Grivas
*Athens 1993*

1 e4 c5 2 ♘f3 ♘c6 3 d4 cxd4 4 ♘xd4 ♕b6 5 ♘b3 ♘f6 6 ♘c3 e6 7 ♗d3 d6 8 ♗e3 ♕c7 9 f4 a6 10 ♕f3 ♗e7 11 0-0-0 b5 12 ♔b1 ♘d7 13 g4 *(D)*

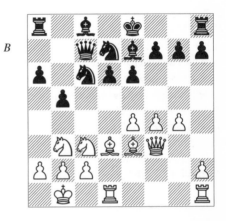

**13...♘b4**

Another promising continuation for Black is 13...♘b6 14 g5 ♘a4 15 ♗d2 ♘xc3+ 16 ♗xc3 e5 17 ♗d2 exf4 18 ♗xf4 0-0 19 h4 ♗e6 = ½-½ Shirov-Grivas, Rethymnon ECC 2003.

**14 g5 ♗b7 15 ♖hf1**

Other ideas are 15 ♖hg1!? and 15 ♕h3 0-0, continuing with either 16 ♖hf1 or 16 ♖hg1.

**15...0-0 16 h4!?**

A new move. White usually prefers 16 ♕h3.

**16...♖ac8**

Threatening 17...♘xc2! and 18...b4.

**17 g6?**

Despite the fact that this standard move helps to open lines against the black king, in this position it is a bad idea as it allows Black considerable activity. White should have opted for the passive 17 ♖c1.

**17...♗f6!** *(D)*

White's intentions would have been vindicated after the mistaken 17...fxg6? 18 ♕h3! or 17...hxg6? 18 h5!.

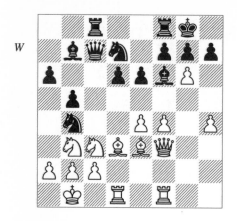

**18 gxf7+**

After 18 gxh7+ ♚h8! Black's king is shielded by the white h7-pawn.

**18...♖xf7 19 ♗d4**

White could also try the interesting 19 ♘d4!? ♛a5!? (or even 19...♘c5).

**19...e5 20 fxe5 ♘xe5 21 ♛h3 ♘bxd3!**

Black weakens White's pawn-structure and takes over the initiative.

**22 cxd3 b4 23 ♘a4 ♗c6 24 ♘b6**

24 ♖c1 ♛d7! 25 ♛xd7 ♗xd7 26 ♖xc8+ ♗xc8 27 ♘b6 ♗e6 leads to an endgame that is good for Black.

**24...♖b8 25 ♘d5 ♗xd5 26 exd5 ♛d7!** (D)

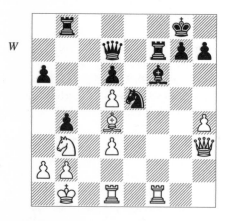

Black would welcome the transition to an endgame, as the superiority of his pawn-structure would become a decisive factor. White therefore feels obliged to seek tactical counterplay, for which all of his pieces are necessary.

**27 ♛g3 ♛b5 28 ♛g2 ♖bf8 29 h5 h6 30 ♗e3**

Toying with threats such as 31 ♗xh6 or 31 ♘d4 followed by ♘f5.

**30...♘xd3! 31 ♖xf6**

Desperation, but other options were also clearly hopeless: 31 ♗xh6 ♘xb2 32 ♖xf6 ♘xd1 33 ♖g6 ♛d3+ −+; 31 ♘d4 ♗xd4 32 ♗xd4 ♛c4! 33 ♖xf7 ♖xf7 34 ♛g1 ♘e5 35 ♗xe5 ♛e4+ −+.

**31...♖xf6 32 ♘d4 ♛c4 33 ♘e6 ♖8f7 34 ♗d4**

White could not have saved himself with 34 b3 ♛c3! 35 ♗d4 ♖f2! either.

**34...♘f4! 35 ♛h1 ♘xe6!**

The simplest. By returning part of his extra material, Black ensures simplification down to a clearly winning ending, thus avoiding any complications that White could hope to benefit from.

**36 ♗xf6 ♖xf6 37 dxe6 ♖xe6** (D)

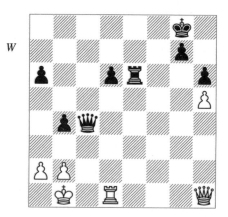

The resulting endgame with two extra pawns has been the logical outcome of Black's correct strategic and tactical handling of the position.

**38 ♖c1 ♛e4+ 39 ♛xe4 ♖xe4 40 ♖c8+**

Or 40 ♖c6? a5 41 ♖xd6 ♖e5! and the win is straightforward.

**40...♚f7 41 ♖a8 ♖e5 42 ♖xa6 ♖xh5 43 ♖xd6 g5 44 ♚c2 g4 45 ♚d3 g3 46 ♚e2 ♖f5 47 ♖d3 ♖f2+ 48 ♚e1 ♖xb2 49 ♖f3+ ♚e7 50 ♖xg3 ♖xa2 51 ♖b3 ♖a4 52 ♚d2 h5 53 ♚c2 ♚f6 54 ♚b2 ♚g5 55 ♖g3+ ♚f4 56 ♖d3 ♖a5 57 ♖d4+ ♚g5 58 ♖xb4 ♖c5 59 ♖d4 h4 60 ♖d3 ♚h5 61 ♚b1 ♚g4 62 ♖d4+ ♚g3 0-1**

White resigned due to 63 ♖d3+ ♚g2 64 ♖d2+ ♚f3 65 ♖d3+ ♚e2 66 ♖h3 ♖h5 67 ♚c2 ♚f2 68 ♚d2 ♚g2 69 ♖a3 h3.

## Grivas – J. Polgar
*Corfu 1990*

**1 d4 ♘f6 2 c4 g6 3 ♘c3 ♗g7 4 e4 d6 5 h3 0-0 6 ♗e3 e5 7 d5 ♘a6 8 g4!**

8 ♗d3?! is clearly inferior due to 8...♘c5 9 ♗c2 a5 intending ...♘h5.

**8...♘c5 9 ♕c2 h5!?**

9...a5 is seen more often here.

**10 g5 ♘h7** *(D)*

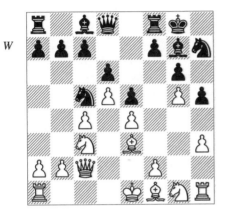

**11 ♘f3**

After 11 h4?! f6! Black obtains targets to aim at.

**11...f6?!**

But now this move is hardly suitable. Black should have opted for 11...f5 12 h4 ±.

**12 ♖g1! a5**

After 12...f5?! 13 ♘h4! ♕e8 14 exf5 ♗xf5 (14...gxf5? is met by 15 g6!) 15 ♘xf5 ♖xf5 16 ♘e4! with the idea of h4 White has a large advantage.

**13 0-0-0 fxg5?!**

Black insists on playing on the kingside, but in view of White's chosen set-up this plan is hardly advisable. Alternatives such as 13...♗d7 or 13...♖a6 and ...♖b6 are more in the spirit of the position.

**14 ♘xg5 ♘xg5 15 ♗xg5 ♗f6 16 ♗e3!** *(D)*

The sequence 16 ♗h6?! ♖f7 17 ♖xg6+? ♔h7 would entirely justify Black's play, while an exchange of dark-squared bishops would weaken the f4-square and practically give up on the idea of ever playing f4.

**16...♔h7 17 ♗e2!**

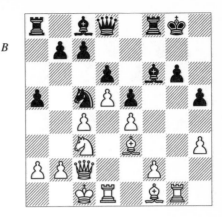

Forcing play with 17 ♗xc5? would turn out to be mistaken: 17...dxc5 18 f4 exf4 19 e5 ♗f5 20 ♗d3 ♗xe5 21 ♗xf5 ♖xf5 22 ♖xg6 ♔xg6 23 ♖g1+ ♔f6 24 ♕g2 ♕g8!. But after the text-move, White's attack arrives much faster than Black's.

**17...♗h4**

White wins after 17...♗xh3?! 18 ♖h1 ♗d7 19 ♗xh5! gxh5 20 ♕e2!.

**18 ♖g2 ♗d7 19 ♖dg1 ♗e8 20 ♕d2?!**

This is inaccurate. White had the strong 20 f4! exf4 21 e5 ♗g3 22 ♗xh5 ♕h4 23 ♗f3 at his disposal.

**20...♕f6 21 f4! exf4 22 ♗d4 ♕e7 23 ♗xh5 g5! 24 ♕e2!?**

The simple 24 ♗f3 would also guarantee an advantage.

**24...♔h6**

Black should have tried 24...♘d3+ 25 ♔c2! f3 26 ♗xf3 ♘f4 27 ♕e3 ♘xg2 28 ♖xg2, though White's attacking chances are more significant than Black's extra material in the middlegame.

**25 ♗f3 ♘d7 26 ♗f2! ♘e5 27 ♗xh4 gxh4** *(D)*

**28 ♘d1!**

White is planning the decisive manoeuvre ♘f2-g4 to exchange off Black's best piece (the e5-knight). Indeed, it is this knight that is holding Black's defence together.

**28...♗f7 29 ♘f2 ♖g8 30 ♘g4+ ♘xg4 31 ♗xg4**

And, as we often say during analysis, the rest is a matter of technique! During a game however, there are also other problems to be solved,

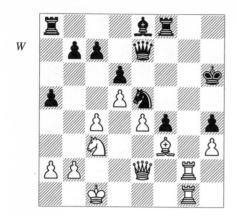

W

such as the 'naturally' severe time-pressure that White was facing at this point.

**31...罝ae8 32 罝e1?**

The simplest win here is 32 豐f2! 豐f6 33 奧f5.

**32...豐f6 33 豐d2 奧h5 34 罝f2 奧xg4 35 罝xf4 豐g5 36 罝g1 罝ef8 37 罝gxg4 罝xf4 38 罝xf4 奧h7 39 奧c2?**

39 罝f7+! is a simple win, unlike 39 豐f2? 豐g1+!.

**39...豐g3** *(D)*

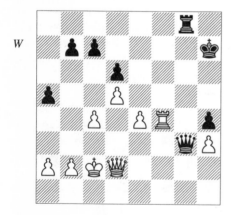

W

**40 罝f6?!**

Again White had to play 40 罝f7+!, maintaining a significant advantage. Now he is left with only a symbolic edge, but on the positive side the time-control has been reached.

**40...罝g6 41 罝f7+ 奧g8 42 罝f2 豐xh3 43 豐f4 豐g4 44 豐f7+ 奧h8 45 奧b3!**

An original and excellent plan. White's king seeks shelter among the opponent's queenside

pawns, where it will also prove very relevantly placed in any ending. The immediate 45 罝f4? 豐e2+ 46 奧b3 豐d1+ (or 46...豐d3+, mating) 47 奧a3 罝g3+ 48 b3 罝xb3+!! 49 axb3 豐a1# would have been a tragic way to lose this game.

**45...罝g7 46 豐e8+ 奧h7 47 奧a4! 豐g6?**

Black had to play the unclear 47...b6! as she would also be lost after 47...豐d7+? 48 豐xd7 罝xd7 49 罝h2!.

**48 豐f8! 豐xe4 49 罝f4 豐c2+** *(D)*

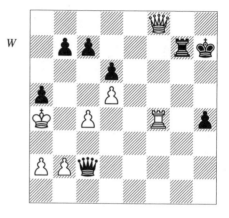

W

**50 奧a3?**

A cowardly move! The aggressive 50 奧xa5! b6+ 51 奧a6! (51 奧b5? c6+!! with a draw) 51...豐a4+ 52 奧b7 would secure victory.

**50...豐d3+ 51 b3 豐g3 52 豐f5+**

White could have tried 52 豐f6! 罝g5! (not 52...h3? 53 罝h4+ 奧g8 54 豐e6+) 53 豐f7+ 奧h6 (53...奧h8? 54 罝f6!; 53...罝g7? 54 豐h5+ 奧g8 55 罝xh4) 54 豐f6+ 奧h7 with equality.

**52...奧h6 53 豐f6+ 奧h5 54 罝xh4+**

White's last try could have been 54 罝f5+ 罝g5 (forced) 55 罝f4.

**54...豐xh4 55 豐xg7 豐e1 56 豐xc7 豐b4+ ½-½**

This game, full of mistakes but also several original ideas, time-trouble, positional and tactical motifs ends, somewhat fittingly, in a draw by perpetual check.

**Grivas – Lputian**
*Zonal, Panormo 1998*

1 ♘f3 ♘f6 2 c4 g6 3 ♘c3 d5 4 d4 ♗g7 5 ♗g5 ♘e4 6 ♗h4 ♘xc3 7 bxc3 dxc4 8 豐a4+ c6?!

The main theoretical move, 8...♕d7, is preferable.

**9 ♕xc4 ♘a6 10 e4!** *(D)*

A new move. White offers a pawn, as the alternative 10 e3 does not seem to promise very much.

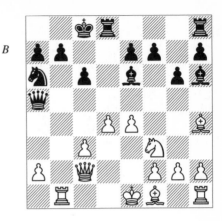

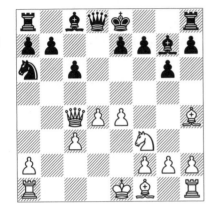

**10...♕a5 11 ♖c1!**

Of course 11 ♗e2? ♗e6 12 ♕d3 ♘c5! 13 ♕c2 ♘xe4! would be disastrous for White.

**11...♗e6**

11...♗g4!? is interesting.

**12 ♕d3 ♗h6**

The a2-pawn was immune: 12...♗xa2? 13 ♖a1 ± or 12...♕xa2 13 ♗e2 ♕a5 (13...♗h6 14 ♗g5! ±) 14 0-0 ♕c7 15 ♘g5! ♗c8 16 f4 ±.

**13 ♖b1!**

The best move. 13 ♖c2? ♗xa2! and 13 ♖d1 ♕xa2 14 ♗e2? ♗b3 are clearly not very helpful, while 13 ♖a1 ♗g7! is nothing more than a move repetition.

**13...0-0-0**

White would retain a big advantage after 13...♕xa2? 14 ♖xb7 ♗b3 15 ♗e2! ♕a1+ 16 ♗d1 ♗xd1 (16...♕xd1+ 17 ♕xd1 ♗xd1 18 ♔xd1 ±) 17 0-0!.

**14 ♕c2!** *(D)*

Another good move. 14 ♗e2? ♘c5! is plain bad for White, while after 14 ♗xe7 ♖d7 15 ♗f6 ♖e8 Black has excellent compensation.

**14...f6!?**

An interesting attempt to find play. Once again 14...♕xa2 15 ♕xa2 ♗xa2 16 ♖a1 ♗e6 17 ♗xe7 would offer White a large plus.

**15 ♗g3!**

White avoids the positional threat 15 ♗e2?! ♗f4! intending ...g5 and ...h5, when Black obtains strong counterplay.

**15...f5**

And once more 15...♕xa2 16 ♕xa2 ♗xa2 17 ♖b2! ♗e6 18 ♗xa6 bxa6 19 ♖b8+ would have been excellent for White.

**16 exf5 gxf5**

White retains his advantage after 16...♗xf5!? 17 ♗d3! ♗xd3 18 ♕xd3 as well.

**17 ♗e5 ♖hg8 18 ♗d3! ♖df8?**

But this is a serious mistake. Black's only real option was to go for 18...♖xg2 19 ♘h4! ♖gg8 20 ♘xf5 ♗f8 21 ♔e2!, when White is much better but at least Black enjoys certain practical chances due to the fact that the white king is stuck in the centre.

**19 0-0** *(D)*

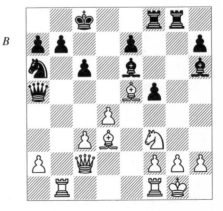

White has now safeguarded his king and is ready to attack its more exposed counterpart. In sharp contrast to White's pleasant task, Black is unable to cause any serious trouble to the white king, which effectively means that he is denied any counterplay. This fact often proves of vital importance in this type of position.

**19...♗d5 20 ♘h4**

A big plus is promised by 20 ♗xf5+ e6 21 ♗h3 (or 21 ♗e4 ♖xf3 22 ♗xf3 ♗xf3 23 ♗g3) 21...♗xf3 22 ♕b3!, but the text-move is also strong.

**20...b5**

Black's alternatives are also unsatisfactory: 20...♖g4? 21 ♗xf5+, 20...♗g5 21 ♘xf5! or 20...♖g5 21 c4, with a winning position for White in all cases.

**21 a4!** *(D)*

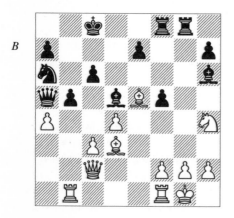

This pawn, which has been on offer for several moves, now delivers the decisive blow on the black king's protective armour!

**21...♘c7 22 axb5 cxb5 23 ♗xc7 ♕xc7 24 ♖xb5 ♗c6 25 ♖c5 ♔b8 26 ♖b1+!**

The best. Things would have been less clear after 26 ♗b5 ♗xb5 or 26 d5 ♕f4.

**26...♔a8 27 ♗b5 1-0**

Black resigned in view of 27...♖f6 28 d5 ♕f4 29 ♖xc6 ♕xh4 30 ♖xf6 ♕xf6 31 ♗c6+.

### Art. Minasian – Grivas
*Ankara 1995*

1 e4 c5 2 ♘f3 ♘c6 3 d4 cxd4 4 ♘xd4 ♕b6 5 ♘b3 ♘f6 6 ♘c3 e6 7 ♗d3 d6 8 ♗e3 ♕c7 9 f4 a6 10 ♕f3 ♗e7 11 0-0-0 b5 12 ♔b1 ♘b4 13 g4 ♗b7 14 g5 ♘d7 15 ♕h3 0-0 16 ♖hg1 ♖fc8! *(D)*

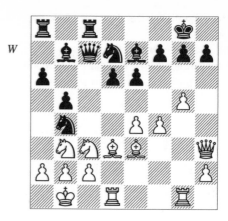

The only good move in this position, and a novelty at the time. Only this move can guarantee the viability of Black's position. All other tries in this position have led to disaster.

**17 ♖d2!?**

White defends against the threat of 17...♘xd3 18 cxd3 b4 while at the same time preparing to double his rooks on the g-file. This, along with the idea ♘d1-f2-g4-h6+, will be the main theme of White's attack. Another possibility is 17 ♘d4 e5! 18 ♘f5 ♗f8! with unclear consequences.

**17...♘xd3 18 cxd3 b4 19 ♘d1 a5!** *(D)*

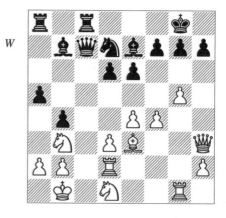

The point behind Black's 16th move. If the attack is going to succeed then all the black pieces must participate. It now becomes clear why Black chose the f-rook: the a8-rook participates both in attack and in defence (it will soon appear on a5), creating dangerous threats, while the advance of the a-pawn will weaken White's king.

**20 ♘f2 a4 21 ♘d4 ♖a5! 22 ♘g4 ♖c5 23 ♖dg2 ♗a6!**

All of Black's pieces are active and create multiple threats, denying White a respite to further his own aims.

**24 ♗d2 a3!** *(D)*

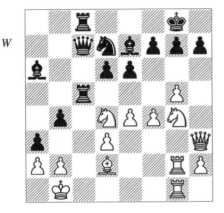

White's position becomes critical. He now decides to complicate matters, hoping for salvation in an attack against the black king.

**25 ♘h6+!?**

Naturally, 25 bxa3? bxa3 leaves the king very exposed, while 25 b3 ♖c3!! is also very troublesome.

**25...gxh6 26 g6**

After 26 gxh6+ ♚h8 27 ♕g3 ♗g5!! (the star rook again comes in handy!) 28 fxg5 ♘e5 White is dead lost.

**26...fxg6! 27 ♖xg6+**

If 27 ♘xe6 then 27...♕b7. Also, 27 ♕xe6+ ♚h8 28 ♕xe7 ♗xd3+ 29 ♚a1 ♖c1+! is decisive as well.

**27...♚h8! 28 ♘xe6?** *(D)*

28 ♕xh6?? ♗xd3+ 29 ♚a1 ♖c1+! leads to checkmate, but White had to try 28 ♖xh6 ♘f6! with enormous complications, though Black's chances ought to be rated higher. One nice variation goes 29 ♘xe6 ♖g5! 30 ♘xc7 (30 ♖c1 ♕xc1+! 31 ♗xc1 ♖g1!) 30...♖xg1+ 31 ♚c2 ♖xc7+ 32 ♚b3 ♖b1!.

**28...♖h5!!**

A brilliant tactical shot, clearing the way for the queen to reach c2. White is lost in all variations.

**29 ♖g8+**

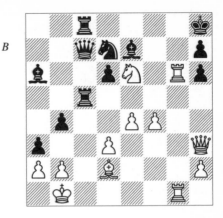

The last – but inadequate – try. Otherwise: 29 ♕xh5 ♕c2+ 30 ♚a1 ♕xb2#; or 29 ♘xc7 ♖xh3 30 ♖e6 ♗xd3+ 31 ♚a1 ♗f6.

**29...♖xg8 30 ♖xg8+ ♚xg8 31 ♕g3+ ♖g5!**

Another easy but nice tactical shot!

**32 fxg5 ♕b6 33 g6**

White prolongs the game only because of the mutual time-trouble, but the result never comes into doubt. 33 gxh6+ ♚f7 is also winning for Black.

**33...♗f6! 34 gxh7+ ♚xh7 35 ♕h3 ♚g8 36 ♕g4+ ♚f7 37 ♘f4 ♘f8 38 ♕h5+ ♚g8 39 ♕d5+ ♚h8 40 ♕f7 ♗g7 41 ♕e8 ♕g1+ 42 ♚c2 axb2 43 ♗e1 b1♕+ 0-1**

## Movsesian – Grivas
*European Clubs Cup, Panormo 2001*

**1 e4 c5 2 ♘f3 ♘c6 3 d4 cxd4 4 ♘xd4 ♕b6 5 ♘b3 ♘f6 6 ♘c3 e6 7 ♕e2 ♗b4 8 ♗d2 0-0 9 a3 ♗e7 10 0-0-0**

One sees 10 e5 ♘d5 more often.

**10...d5** *(D)*

**11 ♗e3!?**

Gofshtein-Grivas, Panormo rpd Ech 2001 proceeded as follows: 11 exd5 ♘xd5 12 ♘xd5 exd5 13 ♕f3!? ♗f6 14 ♗e3 d4 15 ♗f4 ♗e6 16 ♗d3 ♖ac8 17 ♚b1 ♗e7!? 18 ♖he1 ♗xb3 19 cxb3 ♗xa3? 20 ♗xh7+? (20 ♗f5! ±) 20...♚xh7 21 bxa3 ♘a5 22 ♖d3 ♚g8 23 ♗c1! ♖fe8! 24 ♖ed1 ♕g6! 25 ♕g3 ♕e4 26 ♕f4? (26 ♕f3! with equality) 26...♕h7! 27 ♚b2?! ♖e2+ 28 ♖1d2 ♕xd3 0-1.

**11...♕c7 12 exd5 ♘xd5 13 ♘xd5 exd5 14 g4!?**

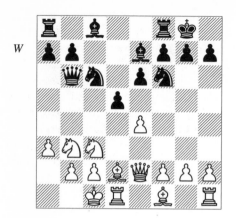

Naturally, 14 ♖xd5? ♗e6 would be a bad idea for White. He could play positionally with 14 g3!? but, quite logically, prefers to try to attack the black king.

**14...♖d8 15 ♗g2 ♗e6 16 ♔b1 ♖ac8 17 f4?!**

An active but dubious move, surrendering the initiative. White should have tried the unclear 17 h3!?.

**17...d4! 18 ♗c1 d3! 19 ♖xd3 ♖xd3 20 ♕xd3 ♗xg4** *(D)*

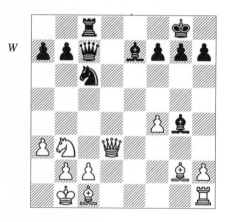

Black has achieved a favourable exchange of his isolated pawn for White's g-pawn. The opening of the g-file is of secondary importance, as White can hardly make profitable use of it.

**21 ♗e4 g6! 22 f5?!**

This looks as natural as a baby's smile, but it actually is the beginning of White's problems. Indeed, my opponent should have given top priority to improving his defences.

**22...♕d6! 23 ♕c4?!**

White should have opted for a slightly worse endgame with 23 ♖g1 ♕xd3 24 ♗xd3 ♗h5. However, it is not easy to make such tough but objective decisions in the heat of the battle with kings castled on opposite sides!

**23...gxf5! 24 ♖g1**

24 ♗d5 ♗f6! 25 ♗xf7+ ♔h8 and Black has the initiative.

**24...♕xh2!** *(D)*

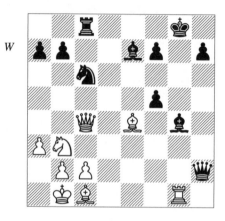

Another seemingly 'illogical' move, the second in a row by Black opening more lines against his king. On the other hand, White cannot breach Black's king shelter without pawns, while Black also strengthens his main defensive bastion, the g4-bishop (...h5 will follow).

**25 ♖h1**

Perhaps 25 ♖g2 ♕h3! had to be tried.

**25...♕c7 26 ♗d5 ♘e5 27 ♕f4 h5!**

Black has a winning position, as well as the usual enemy: severe time-pressure.

**28 ♘d4 ♗f6 29 ♖g1 ♗g7 30 ♖g2 ♘g6! 31 ♕d2**

31 ♕g5 ♕d8!.

**31...a6?!**

31...♖d8! would have won easily.

**32 ♘f3 ♘e7 33 ♗b3** *(D)*

**33...♖d8?!**

A second consecutive mistake. 33...♗xf3! 34 ♖xg7+ ♔xg7 35 ♕h6+ ♔g8 36 ♗g5 ♘d5! (but not 36...♗d5?? 37 ♗f6!) was winning.

**34 ♕f2 ♖d1 35 c3 ♖d7?!**

Black could have won by the straightforward 35...♖xc1+! 36 ♔xc1 ♕f4+ 37 ♘d2 ♕xf2.

**36 ♘g5 ♘d5?**

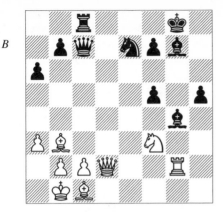

It is only after this fourth(!) mistake by Black that White can finally succeed in (just) drawing the game, a clear indication of how hopeless White's position was.

**37 ♘xf7! ♔xf7 38 ♖xg4! hxg4 39 ♕xf5+ ♔e8 40 ♗xd5 ♕d6 41 ♗e6 ♕d3+ ½-½**

It has become too risky for Black to keep the queens on the board but after the exchanges the ending is a theoretical draw.

### Agnos – Grivas
*Athens 1995*

**1 e4 c5 2 ♘f3 ♘c6 3 d4 cxd4 4 ♘xd4 ♕b6 5 ♘b3 ♘f6 6 ♘c3 e6 7 ♗d3 d6 8 ♗e3 ♕c7 9 f4 a6 10 ♕e2**

One of White's less common alternatives, in place of the standard 10 ♕f3.

**10...b5 11 0-0-0 ♘d7!? 12 ♔b1 ♘b6** *(D)*

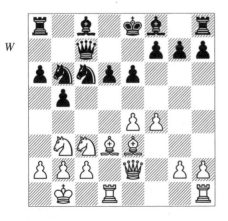

**13 ♕f2?**

An aimless move. White should definitely prefer 13 ♖he1 or 13 g4 ♗e7 14 ♖he1 ♘a4, as in Velimirović-Grivas, Athens 1999.

**13...♘a4! 14 ♘xa4?!**

The opening of the b-file is only to Black's benefit, while the gain of time and destruction of Black's queenside pawn-structure are unimportant. 14 ♘e2 and 14 ♗d2 are preferable.

**14...bxa4 15 ♘d2**

White should probably have chosen 15 ♘d4 ♗e7 16 ♘xc6 ♕xc6.

**15...♗e7 16 ♘c4 ♖b8 17 g4?!**

Simply a loss of time, as White never gets the chance to make use of his kingside pawn advance. 17 f5 is better.

**17...0-0 18 g5** *(D)*

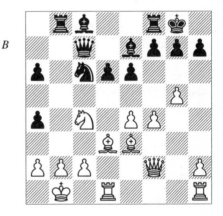

**18...d5!**

A decisive central strike, directly connected with the queenside proceedings.

**19 exd5 exd5 20 ♘e5!?**

Hoping for 20...♘xe5? 21 fxe5 ♕xe5 22 ♗d4, when White finally obtains an attack. However, Black has a very strong sequence at his disposal, completely destroying White's defences.

**20...♕b7! 21 b3 ♘b4!**

With a multitude of threats; for example, 22...♘xa2! 23 ♔xa2 axb3+ 24 cxb3 ♕xb3+ 25 ♔a1 ♕a3+ 26 ♕a2 ♕c3+ and mate follows.

**22 ♗d4 ♘xd3 23 ♖xd3 ♗f5!** *(D)*

Black is winning, as the attack led by his active pieces (the f5-bishop in particular has no opponent) is unstoppable. Even the doubled a-pawns help, as they can deliver consecutive

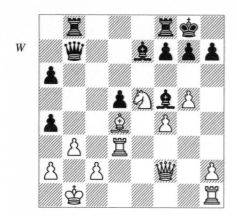

blows upon the spearhead of White's queen-side, the b3-pawn.

**24 ♖c3 ♖fc8! 25 ♖d3**

Pure desperation. In any case, 25 ♖xc8+ ♖xc8 26 ♖c1 axb3 27 axb3 ♕xb3+! would lead to the same result.

**25...a5!**

Opening lines is more urgent than capturing the hapless white rook, which cannot really move anyway.

**26 ♔a1 ♗xd3 27 ♘xd3 axb3 28 cxb3 a4!
29 bxa4 ♕a6! 30 ♘b2 ♗a3 31 ♕e3 ♗xb2+ 32
♗xb2** (D)

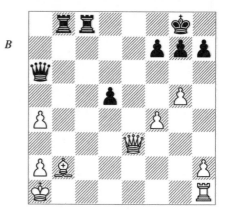

**32...♖c2!**

Black avoids the careless 32...♕xa4?! 33 ♕e5 ♖xb2 34 ♕xb2, when he would still be winning, but would have to work much harder to conclude the game.

**33 ♖e1 ♕xa4! 0-1**

# The Exchange Sacrifice

The positional and tactical element of the exchange sacrifice (rook for bishop or knight) is a very important topic whose exploration requires advanced skills and competitive experience.

This is a difficult subject to master, as the chess-player is required to overcome the dogmatic rules with which he has been brought up, in particular the *quantitative evaluation* of material. The correct implementation of the exchange sacrifice requires an open mind and a proper *qualitative evaluation* of the position.

In many cases the idea of sacrificing the exchange is born out of necessity, prompted by the opponent's threats (i.e. when there is no other acceptable way of meeting them). However, an exchange sacrifice of this kind (passive) does not guarantee positive results, while its failure to meet one's aims (which is quite common in this case) affects the player psychologically and causes him to refrain from such actions in the future.

In the opening and middlegame our pieces should be identified as units that, by cooperating harmoniously, shape our plans, that in turn are executed by means of moves. Each unit is an integral part of our position and we can determine our advantage or inferiority only by taking all units into account.

Naturally, it is not easy to identify which of our pieces (or even the opponent's pieces) carries out the most significant function. We have to take several strategic elements into consideration, such as the centre, open lines, initiative, attack, etc. When carrying out such evaluations, the value of our rooks barely differs from that of our minor pieces, since an advantage is conferred by their fruitful cooperation and not their individual, predetermined, value.

If we accept that, as a rule, the superiority of the rook is realized in the endgame, we naturally come to the conclusion that an exchange sacrifice in the opening or middlegame may be acceptable for many reasons. Before we expand on these reasons, however, we must make an essential differentiation between two types of exchange sacrifices: the *active exchange sacrifice* and the *passive exchange sacrifice*.

The active exchange sacrifice is a rare occurrence and the goals pursued by it are:
1) To exploit our better development.
2) To destroy the opponent's pawn-structure.
3) To open lines in order to attack.
4) To assume the initiative.
5) To control important squares.

As explained above, the passive exchange sacrifice is much more common and may serve the following aims:
1) To repulse the opponent's attack.
2) To repulse the opponent's initiative (a more general interpretation of '1').
3) To destroy the coordination of the opponent's pieces.

As with all such advanced strategic and tactical elements, one factor of great significance is the perception of the right moment to carry them out. The ambitious chess-player must train himself to realize when a situation requires an exchange sacrifice, after properly evaluating the course of the game and the peculiarities specific to the position.

The following examples may offer some proper tuition for our subject, though they still represent only a very small portion of the concept of the exchange sacrifice.

**Dedes – Grivas**
*Khania 1987*

1 e4 c5 2 ♘f3 ♘c6 3 d4 cxd4 4 ♘xd4 ♛b6 5 ♘b3

5 ♘b5 a6 6 ♗e3 is harmless: 6...♕d8 7 ♘5c3 (7 ♘d4? e5 8 ♘b3 ♘f6 9 ♘c3 ♗b4 10 ♕d3 d5!, Rath-Grivas, Munich 1987; Black has a superb game) 7...e6 8 a4 ♘f6 9 ♗e2 d5 10 exd5 exd5 11 ♗f3 ♗e6, Sieverth-Grivas, Munich 1987.

**5...♘f6 6 ♘c3 e6 7 ♗e3 ♕c7** *(D)*

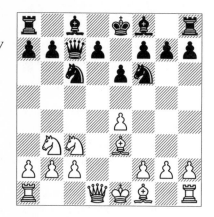

**8 ♗d3**

Among several moves tried in this position it is worth noting 8 ♕f3!? d6 9 0-0-0 a6 10 ♗d3 h5! with unclear play, Gazis-Grivas, Khania 1987, and 8 ♗e2 d6 9 0-0 ♗e7 10 f4 a6 11 ♗f3 ♘d7 12 ♕e2 b5 13 a3 ♗b7 14 ♕f2 0-0 15 ♖ad1 with chances for both sides, Alexakis-Grivas, Athens 1987.

**8...d6 9 f4 a6 10 ♕f3 ♗e7 11 0-0 ♘d7!?**

Not the most common continuation, but an interesting one nevertheless.

**12 ♖ae1 0-0 13 a3 b5 14 ♕h3 ♖e8! 15 e5**

This advance looks dangerous, but in fact only serves to weaken White's centre. In my opinion 15 f5!? and 15 g4 are preferable.

**15...♘f8 16 exd6 ♗xd6 17 ♘e4 ♗e7 18 ♘bc5?!**

Overambitious. Still, Black has no problems after 18 c3 ♘a5! 19 ♘xa5 ♕xa5 =.

**18...b4!** *(D)*

**19 g4?!**

This aimless move significantly weakens the white king. Once again the correct way to proceed was 19 c3!? a5 (19...bxc3? 20 b4!) or even 19 ♕f3!?.

**19...bxa3 20 bxa3 ♖d8! 21 ♕g2 ♘d4!**

The first exchange sacrifice based on the exposure of the white king.

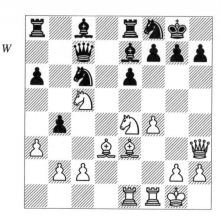

**22 c3**

In fact, White cannot accept the offer: 22 ♗xd4 ♖xd4 23 ♘b3 ♖xd3! 24 cxd3 ♕b6+ 25 ♖f2 ♕xb3 26 ♘f6+ gxf6 27 ♕xa8 ♗b7 28 ♕a7 ♕d5!.

**22...♘b3! 23 ♘xb3 ♖xd3 24 ♗d4**

White could again try to win material, but the consequences would be catastrophic: 24 ♘f6+? ♗xf6 25 ♕xa8 ♗b7 26 ♕a7 (26 ♕e8?? ♗c6) 26...♕c6!. No better is 24 ♘ec5 ♖xe3! 25 ♖xe3 ♗xc5.

**24...♗b7 25 ♘c1 ♖xd4 26 cxd4** *(D)*

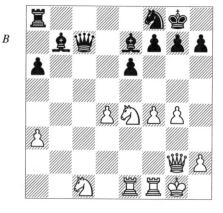

Black's rook has finally managed to achieve its aim! If we examine the position in detail we will observe that Black has obtained some very important gains as compensation for his slight material investment: he has a very solid and sound position, a better pawn-structure, two strong bishops and good attacking possibilities, especially down the h1-a8 diagonal. Moreover,

White's (admittedly slight) initiative has been extinguished, while his pieces are badly coordinated and with no obvious targets. Overall, White's position is very difficult and the practical chances of survival are close to zero.

**26...♖d8**

Black must not rush. The immediate 26...f5? 27 gxf5 exf5 28 ♕a2+! ♔h8 29 ♘g5 ♗xg5 30 fxg5 ♕c6 31 d5! would turn out to be a big mistake. But now the pawns on a3 and d4 are attacked, while 27...f5 is on the cards.

**27 ♕b2 f5! 28 gxf5 exf5 29 ♘g3** (D)

Not, of course, 29 ♕a2+?? ♗d5.

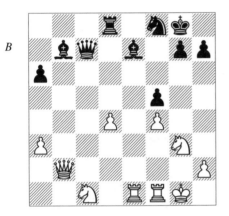

**29...♗f6 30 ♖e5**

No salvation was offered by either 30 ♘xf5 g6 or 30 ♖d1 ♕c6. White returns the extra material in an effort to reduce the force of Black's assault. From a practical viewpoint this decision is correct, but it cannot avert loss as White's weaknesses remain.

**30...♗xe5 31 fxe5 g6 32 ♘ce2 ♘e6 33 ♖b1 ♗c6 34 ♕b6 ♕d7 35 ♕xa6**

White should have tried 35 ♖c1 ♗a8 36 ♕d6 ♕xd6 37 exd6 ♖xd6, although it would also fail to save the game.

**35...♕d5 36 ♔f2 f4! 37 ♘f1 ♘xd4 38 ♘xd4 ♕xd4+ 39 ♔e1 ♕e4+ 40 ♔f2 ♕c2+! 0-1**

### Grivas – Pinter
*Athens 1983*

**1 d4 ♘f6 2 c4 e6 3 ♘f3 d5 4 ♘c3 c6 5 ♗g5 dxc4 6 e4 b5 7 e5 h6 8 ♗h4 g5 9 ♘xg5 hxg5 10 ♗xg5 ♘bd7 11 g3** (D)

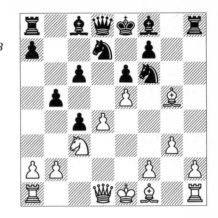

**11...♕a5**

11...♕b6 is considered to be the main line, but the text-move also leads to very complicated play.

**12 exf6 b4 13 ♘e4 ♗a6! 14 ♗e2?!**

The theoretical recommendation here is 14 ♕f3 with unclear play.

**14...0-0-0 15 0-0 ♕f5 16 ♕c2 ♘b6 17 ♖ad1**

Several games have continued with 17 f3!?; e.g., 17...♖xd4 (17...♕h3 18 ♖f2 and ♗f1) 18 ♗e3 ♖d8 (18...c5? 19 ♗xd4 cxd4 20 b3! ♗c5 21 ♗d3!) 19 ♖fd1 ♖xd1+ 20 ♖xd1.

**17...♕h3 18 ♗h4 ♖xh4 19 gxh4** (D)

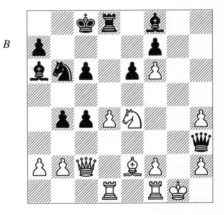

Black has employed an excellent exchange sacrifice, after which his position has several positional pluses: White's pawn-structure is ruined and his king feels very exposed. One should not forget about Black's bishop-pair and the possibility of a knight transfer to the dangerous f4-square. Of course, things are not all rosy for Black: White has extra material and plenty of defensive possibilities, while in an endgame his material superiority would tell.

**19...♗h6 20 ♘g3?!**

White should have played 20 h5! aiming to keep the h-file closed.

**20...♕xh4 21 ♕e4! ♗f4! 22 ♕g2**

The careless 22 ♕xc6+? ♔b8 would only open the long diagonal towards the white king.

**22...♗b7 23 ♗f3 ♘d5 24 ♖fe1! c3! 25 bxc3 bxc3 26 ♘e2?** (D)

White had to play 26 ♖e2.

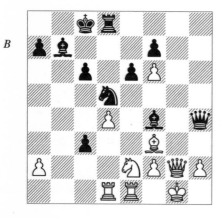

**26...♗d2!**

A strong move, but for reasons neither player grasped over the board. After 26...♖h8?! 27 ♗xd5 ♗xh2+ 28 ♔f1 exd5 29 ♘xc3 ♗a6+ 30 ♘e2 Black retains 'only' excellent compensation for the exchange.

**27 ♖xd2?**

27 ♗xd5 cxd2 28 ♕g3 is preferable.

**27...cxd2?**

The *zwischenzug* 27...♘e3! is strong: 28 ♖c2 ♘xg2 29 ♗xg2 ♗a6! ∓.

**28 ♖d1 ♕h7 29 ♗e4! ♕h8 30 ♖xd2 ♖g8?!**

30...♕xf6 retains the dynamic balance.

**31 ♘g3 ♘f4? 32 ♕f1??** (D)

White should now have continued 32 ♕f3!:

a) 32...♕h6 33 ♗xc6! ♘h3+ 34 ♔g2 ♕xd2 35 ♗xb7+ ♔b8 36 ♔xh3.

b) 32...♘d5 33 ♗xd5 exd5 (33...cxd5 34 ♖b2!) 34 ♖e2 intending ♖e7 and ♕f4.

c) 32...♕xf6 33 ♔h1! (but not 33 ♗xc6? ♘h3+ 34 ♔g2 ♕xf3+ 35 ♗xf3 ♘f4+) threatening 34 ♗xc6 or 34 ♘e2.

d) 32...♘h3+ 33 ♔h1 ♘g5 34 ♕c3! ♘xe4 35 ♘xe4 c5 36 f3!.

In all these lines White has the better prospects.

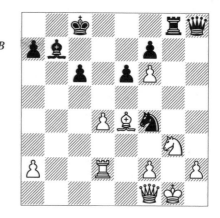

**32...♕h4!**

Threatening to continue 33...♘h3+ 34 ♔h1 ♖xg3!.

**33 ♕e1 ♖h8 34 f3 ♕xf6! 35 ♕c1?**

White should have tried 35 ♔h1!, hoping for 35...♕g5?! 36 ♖c2!.

**35...♕g5!** (D)

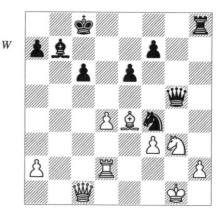

**36 ♕e1**

There was no point in 36 ♕c2 ♖xh2! 37 ♖xh2? ♕xg3+ 38 ♔g2 (38 ♔h1 ♕e1#; 38 ♔f1 ♗a6+) 38...♕xg2+ 39 ♕xg2 ♘xg2 40 ♔xg2 ♔c7 and Black wins. White loses the game because he didn't handle his queen properly! Likewise, 36 ♗xc6?? leads to immediate disaster after 36...♘e2+!.

**36...f5 37 &c2 &f6 38 &c1**

Other moves are no better: 38 &h1 c5! 39 &d1 Zd8!.

**38...&h6 39 &e1 &h3+ 40 &h1 &g5 41 &d1 c5** (D)

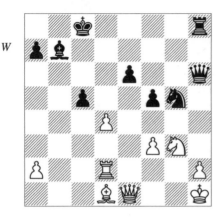

**42 &g1?!**

White's last practical chance was 42 &f1, which is not enough to avoid defeat but at least offers Black a chance to go wrong. Thus 42...&xf3? is insufficient due to 43 &xf3 &xd2 44 &xb7+ &xb7 45 &b5+, when White draws by perpetual check. However, if Black calmly plays 42...cxd4, then he should win, as White lacks real counterplay, and is tied to the defence of his various weaknesses.

**42...&xf3 43 &e5 &xd1 44 &xc5+ &d7 45 &b5+**

Or 45 &xa7+ &e8 46 Zb2 &f3+ 47 &f1 &h3+!.

**45...&e7 46 &xf5+ exf5 47 &b7+ &f6 48 &c6+ &e6 49 d5 Zg8+ 0-1**

### Malakhatko – Grivas
*Athens 2003*

**1 d4 &f6 2 c4 g6 3 &c3 &g7 4 e4 d6 5 &f3 0-0 6 &e2 e5 7 0-0 &c6 8 d5 &e7 9 b4** (D)

Probably the most popular system against the King's Indian in recent years. White immediately commences play on the queenside, where he stands better. On the other hand, Black has plans of his own, particularly on the kingside.

**9...a5 10 &a3**

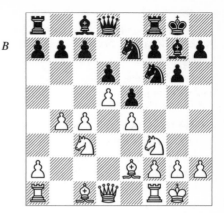

Black's results have been excellent after 10 bxa5?! c5!.

**10...axb4 11 &xb4 &d7**

Sharper lines arise after Black plays ...&h5 on move 10 or 11.

**12 a4 &h6**

12...f5? 13 &g5! would be a criminal mistake.

**13 a5 f5 14 &d3 &h8**

Another option is the immediate 14...&f6 15 c5 (15 &c2!? fxe4 16 &xe4 &xe4 17 &xe4 &f5 is unclear, I.Farago-Safranska, Porto San Giorgio 2002) 15...fxe4 16 &xe4 &xe4 17 &xe4 &f5 18 Ze1 &xe4 19 Zxe4 &f5 20 &b3 b6?! (20...&d7!) 21 cxb6 cxb6 22 a6 b5 23 &c2! &b6 24 &c6 ± K.Müller-Monaccel, IECG e-mail 2001.

**15 Ze1** (D)

White has alternatives in 15 &d2 (Ig.Jelen-Enjuto, Bled OL 2002) and 15 &b3 &f6 16 c5 (I.Jelen-Gabacz, Skofja Loka 2000).

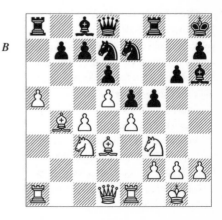

**15...♘f6**

In Gustafsson-K.Larsen, Amsterdam 2001, the inferior 15...♘g8 16 ♘d2 ♖f7 17 ♘a4 ♘df6 18 c5 was played.

**16 c5 fxe4 17 cxd6**

This was compulsory because if 17 ♘xe4, then 17...♘exd5.

**17...cxd6 18 ♘xe4 ♘xe4**

White has a slight but permanent plus after 18...♘exd5 19 ♗xd6 ♘xe4 20 ♗xe4 (20 ♗xf8? ♘ec3!) 20...♕xd6 21 ♕xd5 ♕xd5 22 ♗xd5 ♖d8 23 ♗c4.

**19 ♗xe4 ♗f5** (D)

19...♘f5 20 ♖b1! ♕f6 21 ♗c3 gave White the initiative in Zielinska-Blimke, Brezeg Dolnyi 2000.

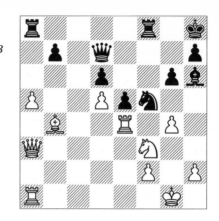

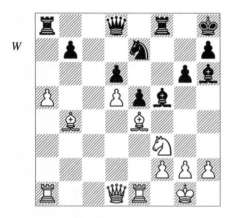

**20 ♕d3**

With threats like 21 ♕b5 or 21 ♕a3.

**20...♕d7! 21 ♕a3**

White could try the alternative plan 21 ♖ab1 and ♗c3, pressurizing the b7-pawn.

**21...♗xe4 22 ♖xe4 ♘f5 23 g4** (D)

White meets the demands of this complicated position and accepts Black's intended exchange sacrifice. After 23 h3 ♖f6!, intending ...♖af8 and ...♘d4, Black's kingside initiative becomes very dangerous.

**23...♘e3!! 24 ♘xe5**

White accepts the sacrifice, which is the correct decision on principle. Instead, White could opt for 24 fxe3 ♖xf3 25 ♗xd6 ♗xe3+ 26 ♖xe3 ♖xe3 27 ♕xe3 ♕xd6 with chances for both sides. Naturally, it was bad to play 24 ♖xe3? ♗xe3 25 ♕xe3 ♕xg4+.

**24...dxe5 25 ♗xf8 ♖xf8 26 ♖xe3?!**

After the logical sequence 26 fxe3 ♕xd5 27 ♕b4 (Black is better after 27 ♕a4 ♕d2! or 27 ♖a4 ♕f3!) 27...♕f7! (27...♕d3!? 28 ♖e1 ♕c2 29 ♖f1!) 28 ♕b2 ♕f3 29 ♕g2 ♗xe3+ 30 ♔h1 ♗d4 the position is approximately balanced. This would have been White's objectively best decision. However, White apparently underestimated the power of the h6-bishop.

**26...♕xg4+ 27 ♖g3 ♕d4! 28 ♖g2 ♕xd5** (D)

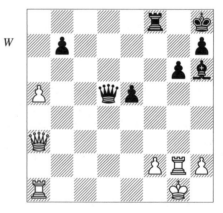

Black now stands better thanks to his healthier pawn-structure, safer king and more active pieces. The h6-bishop can in no way be considered inferior to a white rook, as it has a greater sphere of action and several targets. Even if things don't work out well for Black and he has to acquiesce to several exchanges (queens, one pair of rooks and the queenside pawns) the resulting ending will be a draw. In view of all this White should have avoided this position, where there is danger lurking and his winning chances are almost non-existent, not to mention his severe time-trouble.

**29 Rb1 Rf7!**

After 29...Ra8?! 30 Wb3! Wxb3 31 Rxb3 Rxa5 32 Rg4! b5 33 Rgb4 White would secure the draw.

**30 Wb3 We4!**

A queen exchange at any moment would relieve White. Instead, Black improves his position by making use of tactics.

**31 Rf1 ☗g7 32 We6! ☗d2! 33 Rg4?!** *(D)*

White should have preferred 33 a6! bxa6 34 Wxa6 ☗c3 and ...☗d4, with a slight advantage for Black.

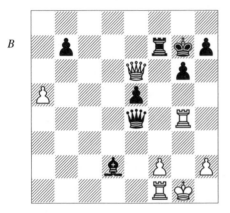

**33...We2 34 Rg3 ☗f4 35 Rg2 ☗d2?!**

After the better 35...Wb5!, intending ...Wa4 followed by ...Rd7-d1, White's defences would be stretched to the limit.

**36 Wa2! e4 37 Wb2+ ☗h6 38 Rg3!** *(D)*

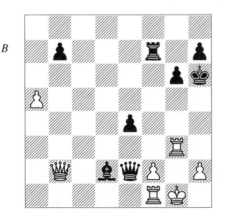

Black is now forced to exchange his rook for the 'bad' white rook on g3, and not the f1-rook which is vital for the defence of the first rank.

**38...Rf3 39 Rxf3 exf3 40 Wxb7 ☗xa5 41 Wb8!**

The white queen returns to the defence in time, securing the draw. Black gave it one more shot due to White's time-pressure, but the position is very simplified and mistakes are difficult to come by.

**41...☗d2 42 Wg3 ☗c3 43 Rb1 We4! 44 Rd1 ☗e5 45 Wh3+ ☗g5 46 ☗h1 h5 47 We6! ☗h4 48 Rc1! Wg4 49 Wxg4+ ☗xg4 ½-½**

## Cheparinov – Grivas
*Asenovgrad 1985*

**1 d4 ☗f6 2 c4 c5 3 d5 d6 4 ☗c3 g6 5 e4 ☗g7 6 f4**

The always dangerous Four Pawns Attack!

**6...0-0 7 ☗f3 e6 8 ☗e2 exd5 9 cxd5 Re8** *(D)*

The oldest line, in which Black encourages White to sacrifice a pawn but for more than sufficient compensation. Most people prefer 9...☗g4.

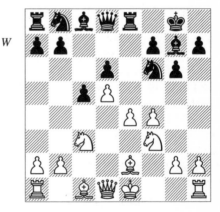

**10 e5 dxe5 11 fxe5 ☗g4 12 ☗g5 Wb6 13 0-0 ☗f5?**

The careless 13...c4+ 14 ☗h1 ☗f2+ 15 Rxf2 Wxf2 16 ☗e4 leads straight to the abyss, but the text-move is also unsatisfactory. The immediate 13...☗xe5 seems best.

**14 d6?**

Black's deserved punishment would be effected by 14 ☗b5! Rxe5 15 ☗xe5 ☗xe5 16

♕e2 ♗xh2+ 17 ♔h1 ♘d7 18 ♗xd7 ♗xd7 19 ♖xf7 ♔xf7 20 ♕e7+ ♔g8 21 ♕xd7 h5 22 ♖f1 ♖f8? 23 ♖xf8+ ♔xf8 24 ♗e7+ ♔g8 25 ♕e8+ ♔h7 26 ♕f7+ ♔h8 27 ♘e4 ♕xb2 28 ♕f8+ 1-0 Utasi-Grivas, Athens 1985.

**14...♘xe5 15 ♘d5 ♕xb2 16 ♖c1 ♘bc6**

Black sacrifices an exchange for good compensation: two pawns, a solid position and active pieces.

**17 ♘c7 h6 18 ♘xe8 ♖xe8 19 ♗h4 ♘d4! 20 ♘xd4 cxd4 21 ♗e7 d3 22 ♗f3 ♗f8** (D)

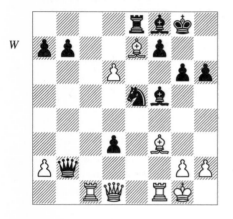

The dangerous white d-pawn must be captured, as otherwise it remains a constant source of counterplay.

**23 ♖c7 ♗xe7 24 ♖xe7 ♕d4+ 25 ♔h1 ♖d8 26 ♖e1! ♘xf3 27 ♖e8+ ♖xe8 28 ♖xe8+ ♔g7 29 gxf3 ♕xd6 30 ♕a1+! f6 31 ♕d1! h5! 32 ♕d2 h4 33 ♖e3** (D)

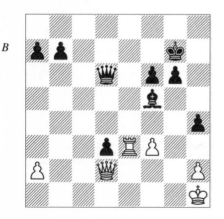

**33...h3**

Black's position is excellent, with three pawns for the exchange and a much safer king. These advantages should normally suffice for the win.

**34 ♔g1 a5 35 ♖e1 g5?**

After the correct 35...♔f7! Black would avoid the queen exchange, which allows White to involve his king in the fight against the black pawns.

**36 ♕e3! ♕d7**

36...♔h6 37 ♕e8! ♕c5+ 38 ♔h1.

**37 ♕e7+ ♕xe7 38 ♖xe7+ ♔f8 39 ♖e1 b5 40 ♔f2 b4** (D)

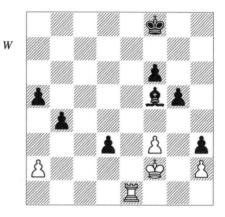

Black appears to have an easy win thanks to his great material plus. However, one should not be fooled by this; with extremely accurate play White can save the draw, making full use of *the great power of the rook in the endgame.*

**41 ♖c1! ♗e6! 42 ♖c5! a4 43 ♖b5**

43 ♖a5? a3 44 ♖b5 b3 45 axb3 a2 46 ♖a5 ♗xb3 47 ♔e3 ♗c4 48 ♔d2 (48 ♖a7 f5 49 ♔d2 g4!) 48...♔e7 49 ♔c3 f5! is losing for White.

**43...♗xa2 44 ♖xb4 ♗b3 45 ♔e3 ♗c2 46 ♖b7 f5! 47 ♖h7!**

The only move. The alluring 47 ♖b5? ♔e7! 48 ♖xf5?? would lose instantly to 48...d2!.

**47...g4 48 fxg4 fxg4 49 ♖h4??**

White stumbles at the last hurdle. He could have achieved his aim with the following line: 49 ♔d2! a3 (49...g3 50 hxg3 a3 51 ♖xh3 a2 52 ♖h8+ ♔g7 53 ♖a8) 50 ♖a7 g3 51 ♖xa3 g2 (51...gxh2 52 ♖a1) 52 ♖a1 ♔f7 53 ♔e3 ♔f6 54 ♔f4! d2 55 ♔e3 d1♕ 56 ♖xd1 ♗xd1 57 ♔f2, reaching a theoretically drawn endgame.

Admittedly, this was very hard to find over the board and required extensive knowledge of endgame theory and exceptional positions, such as this one.

**49...a3 50 ♖h8+**

50 ♖xg4 is not of much help due to 50...a2 51 ♖g1 ♗b1.

**50...♔g7 51 ♖a8 g3! 52 ♖xa3 gxh2 53 ♖a1 d2! 0-1**

After 54 ♔xd2 ♗e4 55 ♔e3 h1♕ 56 ♖xh1 ♗xh1 57 ♔f2 ♗g2 58 ♔g1 ♔g6 the absence of the white h2-pawn denies White the theoretical draw mentioned in a previous comment.

## G. Buckley – Grivas
### *London 1998*

**1 d4 ♘f6 2 c4 g6 3 ♘c3 ♗g7 4 e4 d6 5 f4 0-0 6 ♘f3 c5 7 d5 e6 8 ♗e2 exd5 9 cxd5 ♗g4 10 0-0 ♖e8** *(D)*

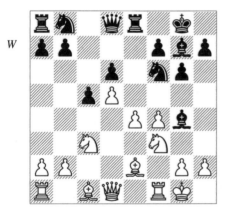

An interesting idea, intending to control the centre by placing the knights on c7 and d7.

**11 h3 ♗xf3 12 ♗xf3 ♘a6 13 e5**

Definitely the critical line. Black faces no problems at all after 13 ♖e1 ♘d7:

a) 14 a3 ♖b8 15 ♘b5 ♕b6 16 ♕a4 ♘c7 17 ♘c3 ♖bd8 18 ♕c2 ♘b5 19 ♘xb5 ♕xb5 20 ♖b1 c4 21 ♗e3 ♖c8 22 ♗f2 ♘c5 23 ♗xc5 ♕xc5+ 24 ♔h2 b5 25 ♖e2 a5 26 ♖be1 b4 27 axb4 axb4 28 e5 dxe5 29 fxe5 ♖xe5 30 ♖xe5 ♗xe5+ 31 ♔h1 b3 32 ♕e2 ♗f6 33 ♖d1 ♕d6 34 ♗e4 c3 35 bxc3 ♖xc3 36 ♖b1 b2 37 ♕xb2 ♖xh3+ 38 gxh3 ♗xb2 39 ♖xb2 ♕f4 0-1 Varelakis-Grivas, Athens 2002.

b) 14 ♗e3 ♘c7 15 e5 dxe5 16 fxe5 ♖xe5 17 ♕d2 ♖xe3 18 ♖xe3 ♗d4 19 ♔h1 ♗xe3 20 ♕xe3 ♕f6 21 d6 ♕xd6 22 ♖d1 ♕e5 23 ♕f2 ♘f6 24 ♗xb7 ♖b8 25 ♕f3 ♘e6 26 ♕c6 ♘d8 0-1 Soultatis-Grivas, Athens 1999.

**13...dxe5 14 fxe5 ♖xe5 15 ♗f4 ♖e7!** *(D)*

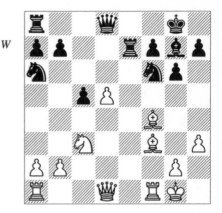

The black rook defends against all of White's threats from the seventh rank, while preparing to attack the dangerous white d-pawn.

**16 d6 ♖d7 17 ♕b3?!**

White should have continued with the unclear 17 ♘d5.

**17...♘b4! 18 ♖ad1 ♖c8!**

Threatening 19...♘d3!! (20 ♖xd3? c4).

**19 ♗e5!? ♘d3! 20 ♗xf6 ♗xf6 21 ♗g4 c4 22 ♕b5 ♖xd6 23 ♗xc8 ♕xc8** *(D)*

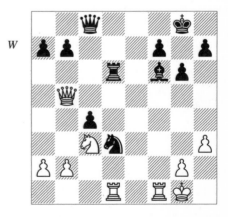

Black has sacrificed an exchange, obtaining two pawns and significant activity as compensation. White's position is critical, so he decides to return the exchange and seek salvation in the endgame.

**24 ♘d5!? ♗d4+ 25 ♔h1 ♕d8! 26 ♕xc4 ♘f2+ 27 ♖xf2 ♗xf2 28 ♕b5 b6 29 ♕d3 ♖e6 30 ♕d2 ♗g3!**

White's position is now lost and indeed he failed to resist Black's threats:

**31 ♖f1 ♖d6 32 ♕c3 ♖xd5 33 ♕xg3 ♕d6 34 ♕f3 ♕d7 35 a3 h5 36 ♕c3 ♖d3 37 ♕f6 ♕d5 38 ♖f3 ♖xf3 39 gxf3 ♕e6 40 ♕d8+ ♔h7 41 ♕h4 ♕f5 0-1**

### Conquest – Grivas
*Afitos 1991*

**1 b3 g6 2 ♗b2 ♘f6 3 g3 ♗g7 4 ♗g2 d5 5 c4 d4 6 ♘f3 c5 7 b4 0-0 8 bxc5 ♘c6 9 0-0 ♘d7 10 d3 ♘xc5 11 ♘bd2 ♖e8!?** *(D)*

A new move. Black usually chose 11...h6 or 11...a5.

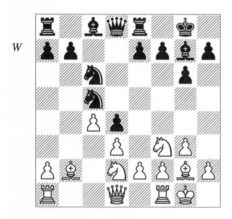

**12 ♗a3 ♕a5 13 ♕c1**

13 ♗xc5!? ♕xc5 14 ♕a4 is an interesting and unclear alternative.

**13...♘a4 14 ♘b3 ♕c7**

14...♕h5 15 ♕g5! with chances for both sides.

**15 ♕c2 ♗d7 16 ♖ae1 ♖ad8!**

Black is now all set to continue with ...h6 and ...e5, developing a strong initiative. White therefore feels obliged to seek complications.

**17 e3 dxe3 18 fxe3 ♗f5! 19 ♘fd4**

This was a must, as 19 e4?! ♗g4 would ensure Black a permanent positional advantage.

**19...♘xd4 20 ♘xd4 ♖xd4!**

A very interesting exchange sacrifice for purely positional compensation (occupation of important central squares and better pawn-structure). Instead, 20...♗d7?! is only equal.

**21 exd4**

White had to accept the sacrifice, as after 21 ♕xa4 ♕d7! Black is clearly better.

**21...♗xd4+ 22 ♔h1 ♘c5 23 ♖d1**

White should have complicated matters further with 23 ♗xc5! ♗xc5 24 ♗e4 ♗h3.

**23...♖d8 24 ♕e2 b6 25 ♗d5** *(D)*

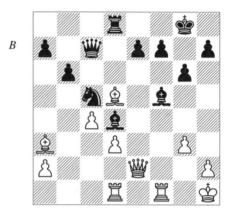

**25...♖xd5!!**

A second exchange sacrifice, only shortly after the first one. This new sacrifice is justified by the subsequently increased activity of the black minor pieces, in sharp contrast to the 'clumsy' white rooks.

**26 cxd5 ♕d7 27 ♖f4?**

White overestimates his chances. After 27 ♕f3! f6! 28 ♗xc5! bxc5 29 ♖b1 ♗h3 30 ♖fe1 ♗g4 31 ♕e4 ♗f5 Black could agree to a draw by repetition, or even perhaps continue trying for a win, despite the fact that materially he is two exchanges down. This proves the validity of Black's earlier choices.

**27...♕xd5+ 28 ♕g2 ♗e6! 29 ♖xd4**

White feels compelled to return part of the extra material as he could find no useful course of action, while Black's threats in the direction of the white king were becoming annoying.

**29...♕xd4 30 ♗b2 ♕d8 31 ♔g1** *(D)*

**31...♗d5?!**

The simplest was 31...♗xa2! and then ...♗d5, with an extra pawn compared to the game.

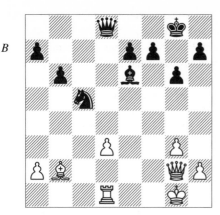

**32 ♕e2 ♕d7 33 a3 ♘e6!**

Threatening ...♘g5-h3+.

**34 ♕e3 f6 35 h4 ♘g7! 36 ♔h2 ♘f5 37 ♕f4 ♕e6 38 ♕d2 ♗c6 39 ♖e1 ♕d6 40 ♕f2 ♕xd3**

Another winning line was 40...♘xh4 41 ♗e5 fxe5 42 gxh4 e4+.

**41 h5 ♘h6??**

Black would win easily with 41...♕d5, intending 42...♘e3!!. With his last move he believed that the win was very near. However, he had overlooked White's next move, after which a queen exchange is forced and results in an endgame where White holds the draw without much effort. A really sad conclusion to a very interesting game with two exchange sacrifices on d4 and d5!

**42 ♕e2!! ♕xe2+ 43 ♖xe2 ♔f7 44 ♖c2 ♗e4 45 hxg6+ hxg6 46 ♖c7 a6 47 ♗d4 b5 48 ♗c5 ♘g8 49 ♖a7 ♗d3 50 ♗b4 ♗c4 51 ♖xa6 e5 52 ♖c6 ♗d3 53 ♖d6 ♗c4 54 ♖c6 ♗d3 55 ♔g1 ♘h6 56 ♔f2 ♘g4+ 57 ♔e1 e4 ½-½**

## Annageldiev – Grivas

*Olympiad, Manila 1992*

**1 d4 ♘f6 2 c4 g6 3 ♘c3 ♗g7 4 e4 d6 5 ♘f3 0-0 6 ♗e2 e5 7 dxe5**

A colourless continuation that fails to trouble Black.

**7...dxe5 8 ♕xd8 ♖xd8 9 ♗g5 ♖e8 10 0-0-0**

Another game of mine went 10 ♘d5 ♘xd5 11 cxd5 c6 12 ♗c4 cxd5 13 ♗xd5 h6 14 ♗e3 ♘d7 15 ♘d2 ♘f6 16 ♗b3 ♘g4 17 ♗c5 ♗f8 18 ♖c1 ♗e6 19 ♔e2 ♗xb3 with equality, Bellon-Grivas, Manila OL 1992.

**10...♘a6 (D)**

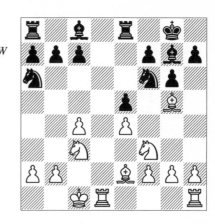

**11 ♘e1 h6 12 ♗h4**

After the inferior 12 ♗e3?! ♘g4! 13 ♗xg4 ♗xg4 14 f3 ♗e6 Black is better thanks to his bishop-pair.

**12...♗e6!? 13 ♘c2 c6 14 ♖d2**

In case of 14 b4!? ♘d7 15 c5 ♘c7 Black would proceed with ...a5 and ...b6.

**14...♘c5 15 f3 a5 16 b3**

Black was threatening 16...a4!.

**16...h5! 17 ♗g5 ♘fd7 18 ♖hd1 f6 19 ♗e3 ♗f8 20 ♔b2 ♗e7 (D)**

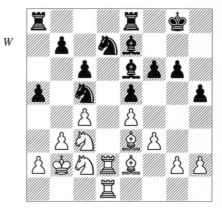

**21 ♘e1**

The position is equal, but the presence of so many pieces on the board promises rich play. For example, White could have gone wrong here with 21 a3?! ♘b6! 22 b4 (White has to try 22 ♘d5) 22...axb4 23 axb4 ♘ca4+ 24 ♘xa4 ♘xa4+ 25 ♔b3 b5!.

**21...♔f7 22 ♔c2 ♖ec8!**

Black is planning ...♖c7, ...♖h8 and ...f5! with the initiative.

**23 ♘d3 ♘xd3?!**

23...♖c7! is much better.

**24 ♖xd3 ♘c5 25 ♗xc5!? ♗xc5 26 ♘a4 ♗d4 27 c5**

27 ♖xd4?! exd4 28 ♘b6 c5! would have been a bad idea, leaving Black better.

**27...♖c7** (D)

Black had no choice as 27...♖d8?! 28 ♘b6 ♖ab8 29 a3! ♔e7 30 b4, intending ♖3d2 and ♗c4, gives White the advantage.

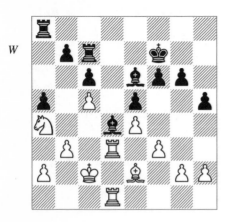

Black's bishops look strong, while the prospect of the position opening up appears undesirable for White. Thus, White resorts to an exchange sacrifice, winning one pawn and hoping for another one (a5) while also assuming the initiative. Meanwhile, Black's rooks seem hardly capable of being activated any time soon.

**28 ♖xd4!? exd4 29 ♖xd4 ♖e8!**

Black must seek activity. The immediate aim is to open lines with the help of ...f5.

**30 ♘b6 ♔g7!**

Intending 31...f5 32 e5 f4! 33 ♖xf4 ♗f5+ 34 ♗d3 ♗xd3+ 35 ♔xd3 ♖xe5.

**31 ♖a4 f5 32 ♔d2 fxe4 33 fxe4 ♖ce7! 34 ♗f3?**

34 ♖xa5? ♗f5! is also bad for White, but he should have continued with 34 ♗d3! ♖f8! 35 ♔e3 ♖ef7 36 ♖xa5 ♖f2, which results in an unclear position. One has to admit though that the black rooks have now become very active.

**34...g5! 35 ♗xh5 ♖h8** (D)

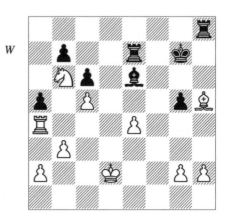

**36 g4**

Black wins after 36 ♗f3 g4 and 37...♖xh2. But now the h5-bishop is cut off from the remaining white army.

**36...♖f8! 37 ♔e3 ♖f1 38 ♔d4 ♖f4 39 ♔d3 ♖f3+ 40 ♔d4 ♖f4 41 ♔d3 ♔f6!**

The timely activation of the black king ensures victory.

**42 ♖xa5 ♔e5 43 ♔c3**

Or 43 ♖a4 ♖f3+! with the idea of ...♖h3 and ...♔f4.

**43...♖xe4 44 ♖a7 ♗xg4 45 ♗xg4 ♖xg4 46 ♘c4+ ♔d5 47 ♔b4**

The result would not be changed by 47 ♖xb7 ♖xb7 48 ♘e3+ ♔xc5 49 ♘xg4 ♖h7 50 ♘f6 ♖h3+.

**47...♖h4 48 ♖a8 ♔e6 49 ♔a5 ♖xh2 50 ♔b6 ♖hh7 51 ♘e3 ♖hg7 52 ♖a4 ♔f6 53 ♘g4+ ♔f5 54 ♘h2**

54 ♘h6+ ♔g6 55 ♘g4 ♖gf7 is also losing for White.

**54...g4 55 ♖d4 g3 56 ♘f3 g2 0-1**

# The Positional Sacrifice

With the term 'positional sacrifice' we imply the surrender of material (usually ranging from a pawn to a minor piece) to the opponent, in exchange for various positional and tactical advantages.

These advantages are classified below (this list in no way claims to be conclusive):

1) Harmonious cooperation of our pieces.
2) Disorganization of the opponent's pieces.
3) Intrusion into the enemy camp.
4) Quick development.
5) Creation of weaknesses around the opponent's king.
6) Possession of the initiative.
7) Space advantage.
8) Other important strategic elements.

The positional sacrifice is an exceptionally deep and complicated element, where objective evaluation of the position and its characteristics is of primary importance. Such sacrifices are usually long-term and the resulting positions are often far from clear. Short-term sacrifices generally have more specific tactical goals, and are termed combinations.

The side making the sacrifice will usually aim to extract from the position the maximum possible benefit, in accordance with the list of advantages above.

The side receiving the sacrifice generally switches to defence. In practice one often sees this side returning the material in order to regain the initiative or simplify into a favourable endgame (or a more simplified position in general).

Naturally, correct judgement and experience aid our decision-making process, but the element of greatest significance is the subconscious collection of 'images' from relevant examples. It is the duty of the chess-player to analyse such examples deeply and invest serious effort in understanding them.

**Grivas – Radulov**
*Athens 1991*

**1 ♘f3 d5 2 c4 c6 3 e3 ♘f6 4 ♘c3 g6 5 d4 ♗g7 6 ♗d3 0-0 7 0-0** *(D)*

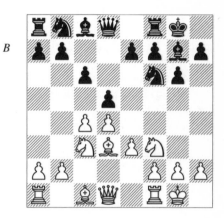

**7...♘bd7?!**

An inferior continuation. Theory recommends 7...♗g4 8 h3 ♗xf3 9 ♕xf3 e6.

**8 h3**

White has interesting alternatives in 8 b3 and even 8 cxd5!?. On the other hand, the immediate 8 e4?! dxe4 9 ♘xe4 ♘xe4 10 ♗xe4 e5 leads to equality.

**8...e6 9 b3 b6 10 a4!? a5 11 cxd5**

White would also be slightly better after the alternative 11 e4 dxe4 12 ♘xe4 ♘xe4 13 ♗xe4 ♗b7 14 ♗g5.

**11...exd5**

11...cxd5? is a mistake: 12 ♗a3 ♖e8 13 ♘b5 and Black is suffering.

**12 ♗a3 ♖e8 13 ♖c1 ♗b7 14 ♖c2 ♘e4**

Black is preparing play on the kingside with ...f5 and ...g5.

**15 ♕b1 f5 16 ♖fc1 ♕f6?** *(D)*

A serious mistake. Black should have continued 16...g5, when after 17 ♗f1 intending 18 ♘xe4 White has just a slight advantage.

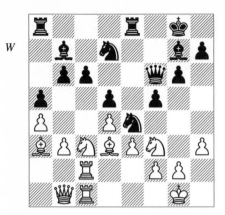

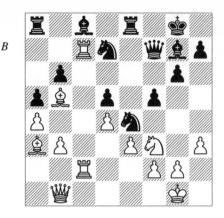

**17 ♘xd5!!**

A positional sacrifice, justified by the following:

1) the harmonious cooperation and placement of White's pieces on the queenside and the c-file in particular;

2) the lack of coordination among the black pieces;

3) the possibility of invading the 7th rank with the rooks; and

4) the participation of all the white pieces (♗b5 and ♘e5 are coming up) in the battle.

Naturally, White's initiative will prove pointless if no material gain can eventually be effected. Such sacrifices are usually based on chess intuition, which is developed slowly but steadily throughout years of study and competitive effort.

**17...cxd5 18 ♖c7! ♗c8 19 ♗b5! ♕e6**

19...♕f7 20 ♖1c2!.

**20 ♖1c6 ♕f7 21 ♖c2!** *(D)*

Black would be let off the hook after 21 ♕c2? ♗a6!.

**21...♗f8?!**

Black's best option is 21...♖d8! 22 ♕c1 (22 ♕f1!? ♖b8 23 ♗c6 intending 24 ♕b5) 22...♗a6 23 ♖xd7! ♖xd7 24 ♗xa6, when White retains obvious compensation for the small material deficit (an exchange for a pawn). Of course, 24...♖xa6?? loses to 25 ♖c8+. Black's position is critical and it seems hard to suggest any decent alternative.

**22 ♗xf8 ♔xf8 23 ♕c1! ♘d6 24 ♗c6?!**

24 ♘e5! ♘xb5 25 ♘xf7 ♘xc7 26 ♘d6! is much better.

**24...♖b8 25 ♕a3 ♕e7 26 ♘e5 ♖d8 27 ♗xd5 ♘e8**

Or 27...♗b7 28 ♗c6!.

**28 ♕xe7+ ♔xe7 29 ♖a7 ♔d6 30 ♘f7+ ♔xd5?!**

Both sides were in time-pressure, which helps to explain the multiple inaccuracies. Here Black should have opted for 30...♔e7 31 ♘xd8 ♔xd8, though White is still better.

**31 ♘xd8 ♘df6 32 ♘c6 ♖b7 33 ♘e7+ ♖xe7 34 ♖xe7 ♗d7 35 f3 ♔d6 36 ♖f7?!**

36 ♖e5! was easy to find and would have concluded the game.

**36...♔e6 37 ♖f8 ♔e7 38 ♖h8 ♔f7 39 ♖b2 ♔g7 40 ♖xe8 ♗xe8 41 ♖c2 ♘d5 42 ♔f2 ♗d7 43 e4!** *(D)*

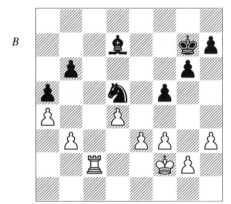

White has finally reached a winning position.

**43...fxe4 44 fxe4 ♘f6 45 ♖e2!**

There was still room for error: 45 ♔e3? ♘xe4!.

**45...♔f7 46 d5 b5 47 ♔e3 bxa4 48 bxa4 ♘e8 49 e5 ♘c7!?**

Black sets another trap. 49...♗xa4 50 ♖a2 ♗d1 51 ♖xa5 is easy for White.

**50 e6+ ♘xe6 51 dxe6+ ♔xe6 52 ♔f4+ ♔f6 53 ♖e5 ♗xa4 54 ♖xa5 ♗c2 55 g4 h6** *(D)*

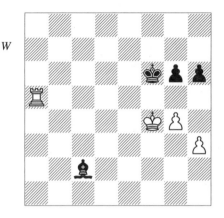

**56 h4!**

If Black were given time to play ...g5 he would reach a theoretically drawn ending. Indeed, the position with white pawns on h3 and g4 and black pawns on h6 and g5 is a draw.

**56...♔e6 57 ♖a6+!**

57 g5 also wins: 57...hxg5+ 58 hxg5 ♗f5 59 ♖e5+ ♔f7 60 ♔e3 followed by bringing the king round to d6 and taking the g6-pawn.

**57...♔f7 58 g5 hxg5+ 59 hxg5 ♗d3 60 ♖b6 1-0**

### Grivas – Popović
*Athens 1990*

**1 d4 ♘f6 2 c4 g6 3 ♘c3 d5 4 ♘f3 ♗g7 5 ♗g5 ♘e4 6 ♗h4 c5 7 cxd5 ♘xc3 8 bxc3 ♕xd5 9 e3 cxd4 10 cxd4 ♘c6 11 ♗e2 0-0 12 0-0** *(D)*

**12...h6?!**

This artificial move is a novelty of dubious merit. Black should have chosen one of the standard moves 12...♗f5, 12...b6, 12...♗g4 and 12...e5.

**13 ♘d2!? e5 14 ♗f3!**

Nothing clear is promised by 14 ♗c4 ♕d7 15 d5 ♘a5 16 e4 ♘xc4 17 ♘xc4 f5 18 f3 b6! with the idea 19...♗a6.

**14...♕d7 15 d5 ♘a5**

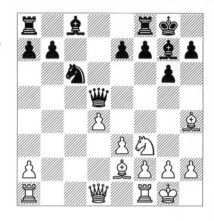

White obtains a clear plus after 15...♘e7?! 16 e4 f5 17 ♗xe7! ♕xe7 18 ♕b3.

**16 e4 f5**

Almost forced. The position after 16...b6?! 17 ♗e2 f5 18 f3 was judged unacceptable by Black.

**17 exf5 gxf5 18 ♖b1 b6**

Perhaps Black should have chosen 18...e4 19 ♗e2 ♕xd5 20 ♘c4! (20 ♖b5? ♕xa2 21 ♗e7 ♗d7!) 20...♕xd1 21 ♖fxd1 ♘xc4 (21...♘c6? 22 ♘d6!) 22 ♗xc4+ ♔h8 23 ♗d5 a5! 24 ♗xb7 ♖b8 25 ♗d5 with a minimal advantage for White. It seems though that he overestimated his prospects – or underestimated the opponent!

**19 d6! e4** *(D)*

There was no choice. 19...♗b7 20 ♗e7 ♖f7 21 ♗xb7 ♘xb7 22 ♘f3! e4 23 ♘h4 ♗f8 24 ♘g6 would grant White a significant plus.

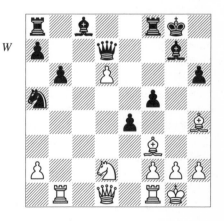

**20 ♘xe4!**

A positional piece sacrifice, for which White obtains the following advantages:

1) two pawns;

2) exposed black king;

3) powerful passed pawn on d6;

4) initiative;

5) harmonious participation of all white pieces in the proceedings.

**20...fxe4 21 ♗xe4**

After the tempting 21 ♕d5+? ♔h8 22 ♕xa8 exf3 Black wins!

**21...♗b7 22 ♖e1!**

All the white pieces are in play!

**22...♖fe8?**

Black falters. He should play 22...♖ae8! 23 ♗e7 ♗xe4 24 ♖xe4 ♖f7 25 ♕d5 ♘c6 26 ♖be1, when White merely has good compensation for his sacrifice.

**23 ♗e7 ♗xe4 24 ♖xe4 ♘c6 25 ♕d5+! ♔h8 26 ♖be1 ♖ac8** (D)

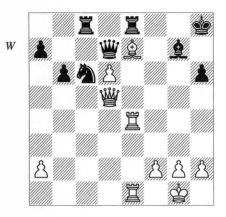

**27 g3**

Perhaps 27 h3 was better, but the choice was difficult to make.

**27...♘b8**

Threatening to play 28...♖c5!. Black's other option is 27...♘xe7 28 ♖xe7 ♖xe7 29 ♖xe7 ♕h3 30 ♕d1! ♗f6 31 ♖xa7 with advantage for White.

**28 ♖e6?!**

Much simpler is 28 ♖h4! ♘c6 (28...♖c5 29 ♕f7 ♖f5 30 ♕g6 and ♖e6) 29 ♕f7 ♘xe7 30 dxe7 b5 (30...♖c6 31 ♖g4!) 31 ♖e6! ♕d2 32 ♖g6 ♖g8 33 ♖e4.

**28...♖c5 29 ♕f3!**

With threats like 30 ♕f7 and ♖xh6+!, Black is unable to stem the tide.

**29...♔g8 30 ♕g4!**

White's threats are too many and too strong (♕g6, ♗f6, etc.). Therefore Black tries his last shot.

**30...♖ec8** (D)

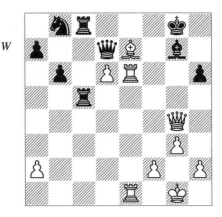

**31 ♗f6?**

Throwing the win away. The correct path was 31 ♔g2! ♖c1 (31...h5 32 ♕g6 ♕e8 33 d7 ♘xd7 34 ♗xc5 ♕xg6 35 ♖xg6 and 36 ♖e7) 32 ♖1e4! ♕b5 33 ♔h3! ♕f1+ 34 ♔h4 ♕xf2 35 h3 and Black cannot meet all of White's threats (♖f4, ♖g6 and ♗f6).

**31...♖c1 32 ♖xc1??**

A second consecutive bad move. Instead, 32 ♕e4! is unclear.

**32...♖xc1+ 33 ♔g2 ♖e1!**

It was this move that White missed; now Black is winning. A sad end to a very interesting sacrificial idea.

**34 ♖e4 ♖xe4 35 ♕xe4 ♗xf6 36 ♕c4+ ♔h8 37 ♕c7 ♕d8 38 f4 a5 39 h4 ♘d7 40 h5 ♕e8 41 ♕c4 ♘c5 0-1**

### Grivas – Espinosa Flores
*Belfort 1983*

**1 d4 d5 2 c4 dxc4 3 ♘f3 ♘f6 4 ♘c3 a6 5 e4**

A very interesting variation, in which White sacrifices material in the fight for the centre and the initiative.

**5...b5 6 e5 ♘d5 7 a4** (D)

**7...c6?!**

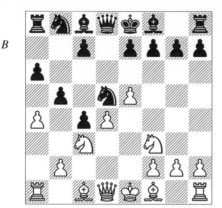

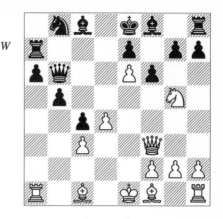

Better options for Black are 7...♘xc3 8 bxc3 ♕d5 and 7...e6 8 axb5 ♘b6, while 7...♘xc3 8 bxc3 ♗b7 and 7...♘b4!? are also possible.

**8 axb5 ♘xc3 9 bxc3 cxb5 10 ♘g5!**

Best, despite the fact that it violates a fundamental opening principle ('do not move your pieces more than once in the opening'). 10 g3 e6 11 ♗g2 ♗b7 12 0-0 ♗e7 13 ♘e1 ♗xg2 14 ♘xg2 ♘d7 15 f4 ♘b6 16 f5 was unclear in Damljanović-Rivas, Groningen jr Ech 1979/80; White's idea can be improved upon though.

**10...f6**

The only move. White was threatening 11 ♕f3 and both 10...e6? 11 ♘xf7! and 10...♗b7 11 e6! would lead Black to a desperate position.

**11 ♕f3!**

The consequences of 11 e6?! ♕d5! (White is on top after 11...fxg5?! 12 ♕f3 ♗xe6 13 ♕xa8 ♗d5 14 ♕a7 e6 15 ♗e2) 12 ♗e2 fxg5 13 ♗h5+! ♔d8! (13...g6? 14 ♗f3 ♕xe6+ 15 ♗e3! ♖a7 16 d5) 14 0-0 ♕xe6 15 ♖e1 ♕f6 16 d5 are unclear, as in Pähtz-Bernard, Rostock 1984.

**11...♖a7 12 e6 ♕b6?!** *(D)*

Black should instead prefer 12...♗b7 13 d5! ♕xd5 14 ♕xd5 ♗xd5 15 ♗e3 fxg5! (15...♖b7? 16 0-0-0!!) 16 ♗xa7 ♘c6 17 ♖xa6 ♘xa7 18 ♖xa7 ±.

White now proceeds with a positional piece sacrifice, by which he reaps very obvious benefits:

1) better development;
2) space advantage;
3) attack on the black king;
4) disharmony in Black's camp.

**13 d5!! fxg5 14 ♗e3!**

14 ♕f7+ ♔d8 15 ♗xg5 ♖d7!! is just unclear, Sosonko-Rivas, Amsterdam 1978. 14 ♗xg5 ♗xe6! 15 ♗e3 ♕b7 16 ♗xa7 ♗xd5 17 ♕e3 is also not clear at all, according to the late Tony Miles. Both these lines are good examples of what we mentioned earlier, about the defender returning the material or sacrificing even more to take over the initiative.

**14...♕c7 15 ♗e2!** *(D)*

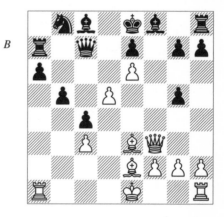

White proceeds with simple developing moves, despite the fact that he has already sacrificed quite some material. However, Black is unable to complete his development and restore coordination among his pieces and, as a result, finds himself in an unenviable situation.

**15...♖a8?!**

Black had to try 15...♘d7!? 16 ♕f7+ ♔d8 17 exd7 ♗xd7 18 ♗xa7 (18 0-0!? ♖a8 19 ♗f3 is also good for White) 18...♕xa7 19 0-0 or 15...♖b7 16 g3 ♗d7 17 0-0 ♔d8 18 exd7 ♕d6

19 ♗xg5, with an advantage for White in both cases.

**16 ♗xg5!**

Threatening 17 ♕f7+ ♔d8 18 d6!.

**16...♕e5 17 h4! h6**

Perhaps 17...♘d7 is a better bet, returning the material with slim chances of survival.

**18 ♗f4 ♕f6 19 ♕g3!**

Threatening 20 ♗h5+ ♔d8 21 ♗c7#. White is now clearly winning.

**19...♗xe6 20 dxe6 ♘c6 21 0-0 g6 22 ♗f3! ♕xe6 23 ♖fe1 ♕f6 24 ♗d5!** *(D)*

24 ♗e5?! ♘xe5 25 ♗xa8 ♗g7 would not have been enough, but 24 ♗d6! is also good.

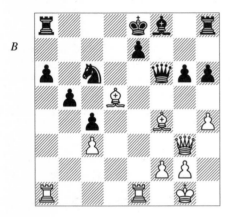

Now the threat of 25 ♖e6 decides.

**1-0**

### Grivas – Zsu. Polgar
*Corfu 1990*

**1 d4 d5 2 c4 dxc4 3 ♘f3 c5 4 e3 cxd4 5 ♗xc4**

White cannot hope for more than equality after 5 exd4 ♗e6!? 6 ♘c3 ♘f6 7 ♘e5 ♘c6 8 ♘xc6 bxc6 9 ♕a4 ♕d7 10 ♗xc4 ♗xc4 11 ♕xc4 e6, as in the game Chekhov-Lukin, Yaroslavl 1982.

**5...♕c7** *(D)*

**6 ♗b3!?**

Most players prefer the less committal 6 ♕b3 e6 7 exd4 (7 0-0 ♘c6 8 ♘xd4 ♗d7 9 ♗e2 ♘xd4 10 exd4 ♗d6 11 h3 ♘e7 12 ♘c3 0-0 = Dizdar-Lputian, Sarajevo 1983) 7...♘f6 8 ♘c3 ♘c6 9 0-0 ♗d7 10 ♕d1 ♗e7 11 ♗g5 0-0 = Dorfman-Lukin, USSR Cup 1984. With the

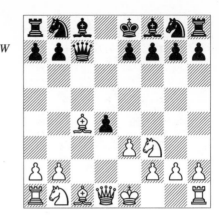

text-move, White sacrifices a pawn for the initiative and a lead in development.

**6...dxe3 7 ♗xe3 e6 8 0-0 ♘f6 9 ♘c3 a6**

10 ♘b5 was an annoying threat, but this move creates new weaknesses.

**10 ♘a4! ♘fd7!? 11 ♘g5!**

The white knights create a host of threats, not allowing Black any respite or choice.

**11...♗e7 12 ♕h5 ♗xg5 13 ♗xg5 0-0 14 ♖fe1!** *(D)*

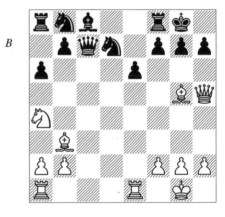

The bishop-pair has been added to White's list of achievements. The battle is now transferred to the kingside, so the rook rushes into combat.

**14...♘c6 15 ♖e3 ♖e8 16 ♗c2?!**

White should have continued 16 ♖h3! ♘f8 17 ♗c2 with a strong attack.

**16...g6!**

Compulsory but also good. Black decides to return the material in order to induce some relieving exchanges. 16...♘f8?? loses on the spot to 17 ♗xh7+! ♘xh7 18 ♖h3.

**17 ♕h6 f5! 18 ♗xf5!** (D)

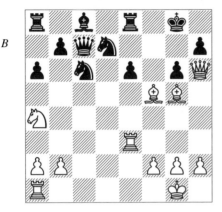

**18...♘de5!**

18...gxf5?? 19 ♖g3 needs no further comment.

**19 ♗h3 ♘f7 20 ♕h4 ♘xg5 21 ♕xg5 e5**

Black is still a little worse but manages to complete her development and things are clearly better than before. The rest of the game is not really relevant to our topic.

**22 ♘c3 ♕d8 23 ♕h6 ♘d4 24 ♖f1 ♖e7 25 ♘e4 ♕f8 26 ♕g5 ♔g7 27 ♗xc8 ♖xc8 28 ♘g3 h6 29 ♕g4 ♖cc7 30 h4 ♕c8 31 ♕e4 ♕e6 32 b3 ♕c6 33 ♕g4 ♕e6 34 ♕d1 ♖cd7 35 ♖d3 ♕d5 36 ♔h1 ♖f7 37 ♕g4 ♔h7 38 h5 g5 39 ♕e4+ ♕xe4 40 ♘xe4 ♖f4 41 ♖e3 ♘c2 42 ♖e2 ♘d4 43 ♖e3 ♘c2 ½-½**

### Velikov – Grivas
*Balkaniad, Kavala 1990*

**1 ♘f3 ♘f6 2 c4 g6 3 g3 ♗g7 4 ♗g2 0-0 5 0-0 d6 6 d4 ♘bd7** (D)

**7 ♕c2**

Another possibility is 7 ♘c3 e5 8 e4; for example, 8...h6!? 9 ♖e1 ♘h7 10 dxe5 dxe5 11 ♕c2 c6 12 ♗e3 ♘g5 13 ♘xg5 hxg5 14 b4 ♖e8 15 ♖ed1 ♕e7 16 ♖ab1 ♘f8 17 ♘a4! ♘e6 18 ♘c5 with equality, Dizdarević-Grivas, Kavala (Balkaniad) 1990, analysed in Volume 3 of this series.

**7...e5 8 ♖d1 ♖e8 9 ♘c3 c6 10 e4 ♕e7 11 b3**

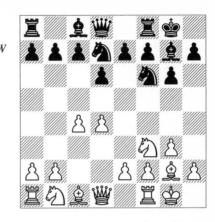

11 d5!? c5 is also interesting when, with the centre closed, the fight is transferred to the flanks.

**11...exd4 12 ♘xd4 ♘c5 13 f3 ♘fd7! 14 h3**

And not 14 b4?! ♘e6, while 14 ♗f4 ♘e5 led to unclear play in Semkov-Grivas, Pernik 1983.

**14...h5! 15 ♖b1 a5**

15...♘f8 is another option, intending ...♘e6, ...h4 and ...g5.

**16 ♘de2!? ♘e5!**

But now 16...♘f8?! is inferior: 17 ♗f4! ♗e5 18 ♗e3 followed by ♗f2 and f4.

**17 ♗e3** (D)

White naturally rejected 17 f4!? ♘ed7! and ...♘f6, with pressure on the e4-pawn.

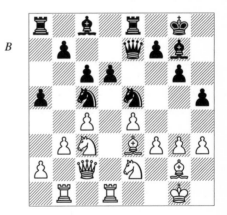

**17...♗xh3!?**

With this very interesting piece sacrifice Black obtains very active play, making a mess of White's position and exposing the white king.

**18 &#9815;xh3 &#9822;xf3+ 19 &#9816;g2 &#9822;g5! 20 &#9815;xg5?**

A serious error. Best was 20 &#9815;xc5! dxc5 21 &#9820;d7 &#9813;e5 22 &#9820;bd1 (22 &#9820;xb7? &#9822;xh3 23 &#9816;xh3 &#9813;e6+ 24 &#9816;g2 &#9813;c8 25 &#9820;b6 &#9813;c7 26 &#9822;a4 &#9820;ad8 27 &#9820;d1 &#9815;h6! with a furious attack for Black) 22...a4! 23 &#9820;xb7 axb3 24 axb3 h4! with complications. Note that 25 gxh4?! &#9822;xh3 26 &#9816;xh3 &#9813;e6+ 27 &#9816;g2 &#9813;g4+! would be most welcome for Black!

**20...&#9813;xg5 21 &#9813;d2** *(D)*

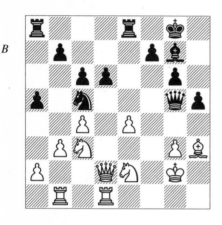

White tries to eliminate Black's most active piece. However, White's problems remain; it becomes clear that he has not evaluated the position correctly.

**21...&#9813;xd2! 22 &#9820;xd2 &#9822;xe4 23 &#9822;xe4 &#9820;xe4 24 &#9822;g1!?**

Continuing the strategy of seeking relief through exchanges.

**24...a4! 25 &#9820;e2**

25 &#9820;xd6 axb3 26 axb3 &#9820;e3! 27 &#9820;d2 &#9815;e5 28 &#9822;e2 &#9820;a3! would not improve things for White.

**25...&#9820;xe2+ 26 &#9822;xe2 axb3 27 axb3 &#9820;a2 28 &#9816;f1 f5!**

Preventing White's liberating intended move 29 &#9815;c8. White is now driven into complete passivity.

**29 &#9815;g2** *(D)*

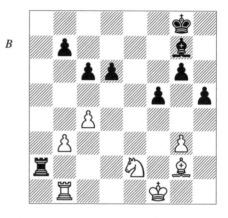

With this move, White sets a trap. Black could have avoided it with 29...&#9820;c2! followed by ...&#9815;e5 and ...&#9816;g7-f6-g5, with good winning chances. Instead...

**29...&#9815;e5? 30 b4!**

White makes full use of the unexpected opportunity and steers the game towards a draw.

**30...&#9820;c2 31 b5! &#9820;xc4 32 bxc6 bxc6 33 &#9820;b6! &#9816;g7**

33...d5? 34 &#9820;xc6!.

**34 &#9820;xc6 &#9820;xc6 35 &#9815;xc6 g5 ½-½**

# Outpost

This element is one of the most often met in practice. The creation and occupation of an outpost plays a significant role in the course of many chess games.

An outpost is a square where we can place one of our pieces without it being attacked by an enemy pawn. Naturally, an outpost gains in value if it is central, and even more so if it is situated inside the enemy camp. The importance of the outpost increases further if the opponent has no bishop moving on squares of the corresponding colour. In most cases it is beneficial to be able to control the outpost with one of our pawns.

Another factor adding value to the outpost is its location on an open file. In that case we are able to double our rooks behind our piece occupying the outpost, and then open the file at the right moment.

The piece we usually aim to place on an outpost is the knight, followed by the bishop, the rook and – in rare cases – the queen.

It follows from the above that a square representing an outpost for us is also a weakness for the opponent and may have seriously negative consequences for him.

In practice we encounter two different cases revolving around the outpost:

1) The outpost has already been created. In this case our task is simple: control it and exploit it.

2) The outpost has not yet been created. This case is clearly more demanding, as we first have to identify which square can serve as an outpost and then try to wrest its control from the opponent. Methods often used in this case are the strengthening of our control of the outpost by pawns and the exchange of those pieces of the opponent that can control it.

Naturally, the possession of one or more outposts does not guarantee victory. The piece that will occupy the outpost will have to cooperate harmoniously with the rest of our army from its powerful position in order to further our aims.

## Bras – Grivas
*Khania 2000*

1 d4 ♘f6 2 ♘f3 g6 3 c4 ♗g7 4 ♘c3 0-0 5 e4 d6 6 ♗e2 ♘bd7 7 0-0 e5 8 dxe5

This tame move does not show any pretensions. White should seek the advantage with either 8 ♕c2 or 8 ♗e3.

8...dxe5 9 ♕c2 c6 10 ♖d1 ♕c7! (D)

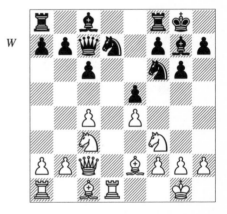

White has voluntarily accepted a weak square in his camp (d4) which, consequently, represents a potential outpost for the black pieces. Black now plans to transfer a knight to d4 via e6. Naturally, things are not that simple yet, but at least Black has a clear plan and White does not.

11 b3?!

Too passive. White should continue with 11 ♖b1 intending b4 and c5 to gain space.

11...♖e8 12 ♗a3?! ♗f8! 13 ♗xf8 ♘xf8

The exchange of the dark-squared bishops is in Black's favour as now the d4-square is even weaker.

14 ♕d2?!

It becomes clear that White is playing without a plan. His only aim is to exchange as many pieces as possible, something he believes will bring the game to a drawish conclusion. In what follows, Black makes full use of this mistaken strategy. White should in any case have played 14 h3! to prevent Black's next move, which is an essential link in his plan.

**14...♗g4!**

The f3-knight controls d4, so it must be exchanged.

**15 ♕d6 ♕xd6 16 ♖xd6 ♔g7!**

The careless 16...♗xf3? 17 ♖xf6! would ruin all of Black's efforts.

**17 ♔f1**

White cannot play 17 ♘d2? ♖ad8! 18 ♖xd8 ♖xd8 19 ♗xg4 ♖xd2! as then Black retains all his former advantages, having also obtained possession of the d-file and the second rank.

**17...♗xf3! 18 ♗xf3 ♘e6 19 ♖dd1 ♘d4** *(D)*

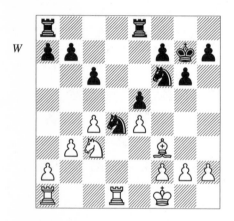

Black has completed his plan and occupied the outpost on d4. Moreover, he preserves the better minor pieces: White's bishop is bad. However, in order to improve his position further, Black has to initiate play on at least one of the flanks, aiming eventually to invade the white ranks through there.

**20 ♗e2 ♘d7 21 ♖ac1 ♘c5**

21...a5?! would be pointless due to 22 ♘a4!, allowing White decent counterplay for no reason whatsoever.

**22 f3**

After 22 b4 ♘ce6, Black will continue with 23...a5!. This will either open the a-file for the

black rooks or force the surrender of the c5-square to the mercy of the black knights (after 24 b5).

**22...a5! 23 ♔f2 f5!**

Since for the moment it proves impossible to open a file on the queenside, Black changes tack and switches his attention to the other flank. The plan is to gain space with ...f4 and then advance the remaining kingside pawns. The end result of this operation will be to open one of the g- and h-files.

**24 ♗d3?!** *(D)*

White's last mistake. Instead, he had to counter Black's above-mentioned plan and seek counterplay in an *unbalanced pawn-structure*. Thus, the indicated choice was 24 exf5! gxf5 25 f4!? ♘xe2 (transforming one strategic element, the outpost, into another – a passed pawn) 26 ♘xe2 e4. Black's advantage remains but White retains much better saving chances, especially if he can engineer the g4 advance under favourable circumstances.

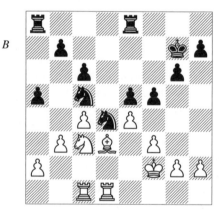

**24...f4! 25 ♘e2 ♖ed8 26 ♘xd4 ♖xd4 27 ♔e2 g5 28 ♗b1 ♘e6!**

The exchange of one pair of rooks is favourable for Black. When a flank file is finally opened and the black rook invades, White will be unable to protect all his weaknesses due to the reduced material.

**29 ♖xd4 ♘xd4+ 30 ♔d2 h5! 31 h3 g4!**

Black is ready to open a file at the appropriate moment. Then he will invade White's camp and exert unbearable pressure. The position is lost for White, who behaved very unambitiously:

always and only seeking exchanges, of which Black accepted only the ones which were in his favour.

**32 fxg4 hxg4 33 hxg4 ♖h8 34 ♖g1 ♖h4 35 g5 ♖g4 36 ♗d3? ♘f3+ 37 gxf3 ♖xg1 38 a4 ♔g6 39 ♗e2 ♔xg5 40 ♔c3 c5 0-1**

### Grivas – Halldorsson
*Reykjavik 1994*

**1 d4 f5 2 ♘f3 ♘f6 3 g3 e6 4 ♗g2 d5?! 5 b3!** *(D)*

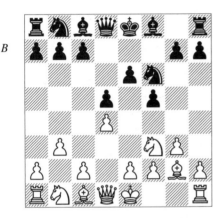

In this move-order White succeeds in forcing the exchange of dark-squared bishops, which is very relevant to the existence of a potential outpost on e5. Black should prefer 4...c6 and then 5...d5. In this particular system, the Stonewall Dutch, Black consciously weakens the e5-square in exchange for strong central control and attacking chances on the kingside.

**5...c6**

Another option is 5...♗d6 6 ♗a3 (Black was threatening 6...♕e7) 6...♗xa3 7 ♘xa3 c5 8 0-0 ♕a5 9 ♘b1! 0-0 10 c4 dxc4 11 ♘bd2! ± Grivas-Karapanos, Nikiti 1990.

**6 0-0 ♗e7 7 ♗a3 0-0 8 c4 ♘bd7 9 ♕c2 ♗xa3 10 ♘xa3 ♕e7 11 ♕b2!**

White strengthens his control over e5 even more, supports the loose a3-knight and prepares (eventually) the advance b4-b5. What more can one ask of a queen?

**11...b6 12 ♖ac1 ♗b7 13 ♘c2!**

Intending ♘e1-d3, contributing to the control of e5. White is slightly better as he has at

his disposal a concrete plan, namely to exploit the outpost on e5.

**13...♘e4 14 ♘ce1** *(D)*

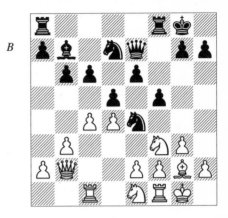

**14...♘g5?!**

As in the previous example, exchanges do not help Black's cause. 14...g5!? is preferable, seeking complications.

**15 ♘xg5 ♕xg5 16 ♘d3 ♕e7 17 b4! ♖fc8 18 a4 a5 19 b5! c5 20 ♖fd1!** *(D)*

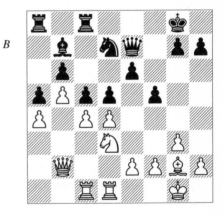

White's superiority is obvious. He commands more space, his minor pieces are better placed and the outpost on e5 is at his mercy. The eventual opening of the position favours White who, by having occupied more space, is better prepared to undertake action.

**20...♖c7**

Black loses at least one pawn after 20...cxd4 21 cxd5 ♗xd5 (21...e5?? 22 d6) 22 ♗xd5 exd5 23 ♕xd4 ♕d6 24 ♘f4.

**21 dxc5 ♘xc5**

21...bxc5? 22 cxd5 exd5 23 ♘f4! leads to the collapse of Black's position.

**22 ♘xc5 ♖xc5 23 cxd5 ♗xd5 24 ♖xc5 ♗xg2?**

Black cannot avoid loss of material after 24...♕xc5 25 ♕e5! (outpost!), but this was surely better than the text-move.

**25 ♖cc1 ♗d5 26 ♕e5! ♖d8 27 ♖c7 ♕g5 28 e4 ♕g4 29 f3 ♕g5 30 exd5 1-0**

## Grivas – Haritakis
*Athens 1989*

**1 c4 e6 2 ♘f3 d5 3 e3**

White chooses a calm opening set-up, preferring to transfer the weight of the struggle to the middlegame.

**3...c6 4 b3 ♘d7 5 ♗b2 f5?!** *(D)*

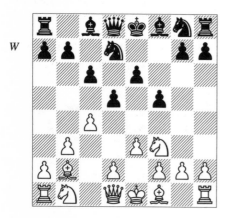

This advance is premature. Black wishes to adopt the Stonewall formation but White has not played d4 yet, and thus the usual positive features (such as control of the e4-square) do not apply.

**6 ♕c2**

Threatening to open the c-file with 7 cxd5.

**6...♘df6!? 7 ♗e2 ♗d6 8 d3!**

Intending 9 ♘bd2 and 10 e4!, which would demolish Black's central structure. In turn, Black finds the only way to try to enforce the advance ...e5.

**8...♕e7! 9 ♗e5!**

The battle for the e5-square is heating up. White makes a preliminary exchange of the dark-squared bishops, thus making e5 more accessible to his knight.

**9...♘h6 10 0-0 ♘f7 11 ♗xd6 ♕xd6 12 ♘c3 0-0**

12...e5?! is premature in view of the variation 13 cxd5 ♘xd5 (13...cxd5?? 14 ♘b5) 14 ♘xd5 ♕xd5 (14...cxd5 15 ♖ac1 0-0 16 ♕c7!) 15 d4! e4 16 ♗c4 ♕d6 17 ♗xf7+ ♔xf7 18 ♘e5+ ±.

**13 ♖ac1 ♗d7**

By controlling the b5-square Black now threatens 14...e5 15 cxd5 cxd5. White has no choice.

**14 d4! ♔h8 15 ♖fd1 ♘e4 16 ♘e1!** *(D)*

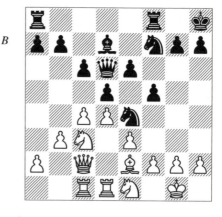

Initiating an unusual plan, the outlines of which are as follows: White will continue with f4 and ♘d3-e5, when Black will, sooner or later, have to exchange the white knight. White will recapture with the f-pawn and then develop his initiative on the queenside. At the most suitable moment White will play cxd5, leaving Black with a choice between ...exd5, when White will have a protected passed pawn on e5 and the clear plan of a minority attack on the queenside, and ...cxd5, when White will invade down the c-file. In both cases White's advantage will be augmented by his space advantage and better bishop. This seemingly simple plan is very strong, and Black finds it very hard to meet it as he is reduced to passivity.

**16...♘fg5?! 17 ♘d3 ♖f6 18 f4 ♘f7 19 ♘e5 ♕e7 20 ♖f1!**

Prophylaxis directed towards a possible ...f4 advance by Black after the exchange on e5.

**20...罝c8** (D)

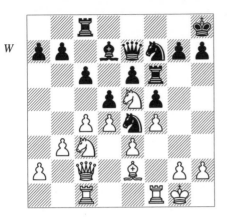

**21 臭d3!**

And this move forces the exchange of knights on c3, because White threatens 22 臭xe4 followed by ⃞xf7+, after which he would have a far superior minor piece (good knight vs bad bishop).

**21...⃞xc3 22 豐xc3 ⃞xe5 23 fxe5 罝ff8 24 b4!**

White's play proceeds according to plan. Black's main problem is lack of any active possibilities.

**24...g5 25 豐d2! 罝f7 26 cxd5! exd5**

26...cxd5 27 罝xc8+ 臭xc8 28 罝c1 is also quite unpleasant for Black.

**27 罝f2 罝cf8 28 罝cf1 臭e6 29 g3**

White does not hurry. It is essential to prevent any possible counterplay by Black involving ...f4.

**29...堂g7 30 a3 h6 31 豐c2 豐d7** (D)

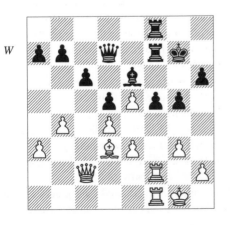

White has an obvious advantage, based on concrete factors: a protected passed pawn (the result of the transformation of a strong outpost), the better bishop and a queenside initiative. Black cannot interfere with White's plan and therefore fails to put up strong resistance.

**32 a4! a6 33 b5 axb5 34 axb5 h5?!**

A desperate attempt at counterplay, ultimately succeeding only in weakening the dark squares around the black king. Although it was tough for Black to accept the passivity of his position, he should have just waited, hoping for mistakes on White's part. By the way, 34...cxb5 35 豐b1! would not help: the pawns on b7 and d5 are very weak.

**35 bxc6 bxc6 36 罝c1 罝c8 37 豐d1! 堂h6 38 臭e2!**

Expecting 38...g4 (which puts an end to any hopes Black might have had to confuse the issue with ...f4) 39 臭d3!, intending 豐a4 and 罝fc2. Black, not willing to acquiesce to the inevitable, decides to commit suicide instead.

**38...h4? 39 gxh4 gxh4 40 罝f4! 罝g7+ 41 堂h1 罝g6 42 豐e1! 堂g7 43 豐xh4 c5 44 罝g1!**

An attack on the exposed black king is the fastest route to victory.

**44...罝xg1+ 45 堂xg1 罝g8 46 豐f6+ 堂h7+ 47 堂f2 罝g7 48 罝h4+ 堂g8 49 罝h6! 1-0**

Remarkably, the e6-bishop is lost!

## Grivas – Blatny
*European Team Ch, Haifa 1989*

**1 d4 ⃞f6 2 ⃞f3 e6 3 臭g5 d5 4 e3 ⃞bd7 5 ⃞bd2 臭e7**

5...c5 6 c3 豐b6 7 罝b1! is another common continuation.

**6 臭d3 c5 7 c3 c4!?**

A new idea. 7...b6 is more standard in this position.

**8 臭c2 b5** (D)

Gaining space on the queenside, where Black plans to play.

**9 0-0**

9 e4?! dxe4 10 ⃞xe4 臭b7 would justify Black's opening play, leading to equality.

**9...臭b7 10 ⃞e5!**

White's only active plan is to play this move and follow up with 11 f4, obtaining excellent

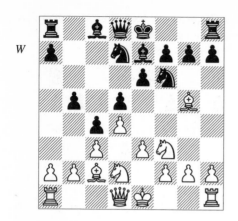

attacking chances. Black practically has no choice other than to exchange the knight, but this offers White a nice outpost on d4.

**10...♘xe5 11 dxe5 ♘d7**

11...♘e4? is out of the question due to 12 ♗xe7 ♕xe7 13 ♘xe4 dxe4 14 ♕g4!.

**12 ♗f4**

White would in general prefer to exchange the dark-squared bishops in order to strengthen the outpost, but here 12 ♗xe7 ♕xe7 13 f4 f6!? would give Black counterplay.

**12...a5 13 ♘f3 ♕b6 14 ♘d4** *(D)*

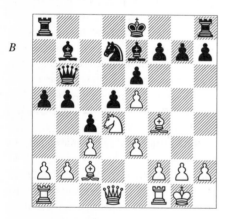

White created an outpost on d4 and has already occupied it with his knight. This piece, in cooperation with the rest of White's army, can help develop a powerful kingside initiative. White is definitely better as Black cannot exchange this strong knight (...♗c5xd4 would negate the outpost but surrender the bishop-pair).

**14...♘c5**

Black cannot continue 14...♘b8? (intending 15...♘c6) because of 15 ♘xb5!.

**15 ♗g3!**

With threats such as 16 f4 (and f5) or 16 ♕g4. The immediate 15 ♕g4?? would lose a piece to 15...g5! 16 ♗g3 (16 ♗xg5 ♖g8 17 h4 h6) 16...h5 17 ♕e2 h4.

**15...0-0**

Black had no other useful move. For example, in case of 15...♘e4? 16 ♘xb5! ♗a6 17 ♘d4 ♕xb2 18 ♗xe4 dxe4 19 ♕a4+ ♔f8 20 ♖ab1! White wins.

**16 ♕h5 ♘e4?!**

Black should have resigned himself to an inferior position with 16...g6 17 ♕h6 ♖fe8. White now increases his advantage by further strengthening his outpost.

**17 ♗h4! ♗xh4 18 ♕xh4 f5** *(D)*

Forced in view of the threatened 19 f3.

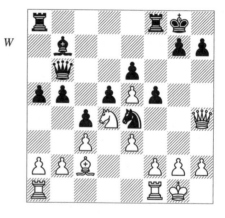

**19 f4! b4 20 ♗xe4! dxe4**

20...fxe4 would have been worse. At least now Black has obtained the d5-square for his bishop, although of course this can hardly compensate for the powerful d4-knight!

**21 ♖f2 ♗d5 22 g4!**

Just like in the previous examples, White develops an initiative on a flank.

**22...♕d8 23 ♕h3?!**

Better was 23 ♕xd8 ♖axd8 24 gxf5 exf5 25 ♖d1 with a technically won ending.

**23...fxg4 24 ♕xg4 ♕e7 25 ♔h1 ♔h8 26 ♖g1 ♖f7 27 ♕h5 ♖af8 28 h3**

Both sides have gathered their pieces on the kingside, White intending to attack there and

Black hoping to defend accordingly. White's position remains preferable.

**28...a4!? 29 cxb4 ♕xb4 30 a3 ♕e7** *(D)*

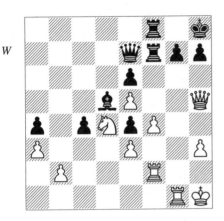

Black has weakened some more squares in his attempts at counterplay, most significantly c3 and d6. White should switch the knight to a different outpost, not necessarily because the new one is of greater importance but because in this way he would restrain Black's activity.

**31 ♖fg2??**

It follows that the correct continuation here is 31 ♘e2 (or 31 ♘b5 planning ♘c3 or ♘d6) followed by doubling rooks on the d-file. Note that Black cannot employ the tactical shot 31...♖f5 32 ♕g4! ♖xe5 due to 33 ♖fg2!.

**31...c3!**

Black obtains a passed a-pawn, which in itself constitutes sufficient counterplay and can prove very dangerous. White has lost his advantage.

**32 bxc3 ♕xa3 33 ♘b5 ♕e7??**

A tragic mistake in time-pressure. After the correct 33...♕c5! 34 c4! ♗c6 35 ♘d6 ♖a7 36 ♖xg7!! ♖xg7 37 ♖xg7 ♔xg7 38 ♕g5+ ♔h8 39 ♕e7! ♔g8! 40 ♕g5+ the game would end in a draw. But now Black goes down quickly.

**34 ♘d6 ♖f5 35 ♘xf5 ♖xf5 36 ♕e2 g6 37 c4 ♗c6 38 ♖d1 ♕h4 39 ♕g4 ♕e7 40 ♖d6 ♕c7 41 ♕h4 ♔g7 42 ♖xe6 ♖f7 43 f5 1-0**

## Grivas – Goldberg
*Dresden 2002*

**1 c4 e5 2 ♘c3 ♘f6 3 ♘f3 ♘c6 4 g3 d5 5 cxd5 ♘xd5 6 ♗g2 ♘b6 7 0-0 ♗e7 8 b3!?** *(D)*

An interesting continuation, in place of the common and worn-out 8 d3.

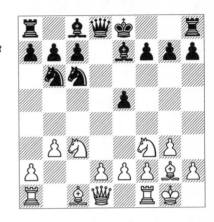

**8...0-0 9 ♗b2 ♗g4 10 ♖c1 f5 11 d3 ♗f6**

11...a5 is an alternative, preventing the following move by White.

**12 b4!? ♘d4**

Naturally, 12...♘xb4?? 13 ♕b3+ ♘4d5 14 e4 was not on but Black should have perhaps preferred 12...a6 13 e3!, with chances for both sides in a complicated position.

**13 ♘d2!?**

With this move White initiates a 'positional combination' aiming to create an outpost on e4 and occupy it. The idea behind this operation is well known and arises in several positions of this type from various openings. One characteristic example is Apicella-Svidler, Erevan OL 1996, which commenced with the Sicilian Defence: 1 e4 c5 2 ♘f3 ♘c6 3 d4 cxd4 4 ♘xd4 ♘f6 5 ♘c3 d6 6 ♗e2 g6 7 0-0 ♗g7 8 ♘b3 0-0 9 ♗g5 a6 10 f4 b5 11 ♗f3 ♗b7 12 ♔h1 ♘d7 13 ♖b1 ♖e8 14 ♘d5 f6 15 ♗h4 e6 16 ♘e3 g5 17 ♗g3 gxf4 18 ♗xf4 ♘de5 19 ♗h5 ♖f8 20 c3 ♕e7 21 ♕e2 ♘g6 22 ♗g3 ♘ce5 23 ♘d2 ♔h8 24 ♖f2 ♖ad8 25 ♖bf1 ♗h6 26 ♘g4 ♘xg4 27 ♗xg4 d5 28 ♗h5 dxe4 29 ♘xe4 f5 30 ♗xg6 hxg6 31 ♘d6 ♗a8 32 ♗e5+ ♔g8 33 ♖d1 ♖d7 34 ♕d3 ♖fd8 35 ♕g3 ♕g5 36 ♕xg5 ♗xg5 37 ♖d3 ♗e4 38 ♖h3 ♖xd6 39 ♖h8+ ♔f7 40 ♖h7+ ♔e8 41 ♖h8+ ♔d7 0-1.

The standard continuation is 13 ♘xd4 exd4 14 ♘a4 ♘xa4 15 ♕xa4 c6 16 ♕b3+ ♔h8 17 ♖fe1 with approximately even chances.

**13...c6 14 f3! ♗h5 15 e3 ♘e6 16 g4! ♗g6**

Black could also try 16...♕xd3 17 gxh5 ♕xe3+ 18 ♔h1 ♘f4 with a complicated position.

**17 gxf5 ♗xf5 18 ♘de4** *(D)*

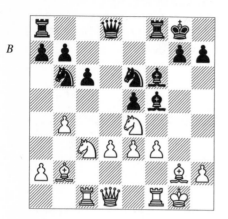

White has completed his plan with success. The e4-square has been turned into a strong outpost, but Black is not without chances either, particularly in view of White's somewhat weakened pawn-structure.

**18...♗e7! 19 b5!?**

White could also try 19 a3 a5 20 bxa5 ♖xa5 21 ♕b3 with unclear play.

**19...cxb5**

The critical move. 19...c5 leads to unclear play and is also possible. Black's move in the game is the beginning of a tactical plan.

**20 ♘xb5 ♘d5**

With the double threat of 21...♘xe3 and 21...♕b6.

**21 ♕b3!**

White had foreseen this before he played his 19th move. Black is now caught in a nasty pin.

**21...♘xe3 22 ♘c7 ♘xf1 23 ♗xf1**

Not, of course, 23 ♘xe6? ♕b6+ 24 ♕xb6 axb6 25 ♘xf8 ♘e3 26 ♘g3 ♔xf8 27 ♘xf5 ♘xf5, when Black is doing well.

**23...♕d7** *(D)*

**24 ♘g3?**

White overestimates his position. He should have chosen 24 ♘xa8 ♖xa8 25 ♗xe5 with an unclear game.

**24...♔h8**

Both 24...♗g6?? 25 ♗h3! and 24...♖ac8?? 25 ♘xf5 ♖xc7 (25...♖xf5 26 ♘xe6!) 26 ♖xc7

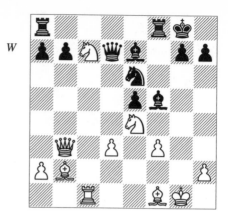

♕xc7 27 ♕xe6+ lose quickly. However, Black could play 24...♗g5! 25 ♖c2 ♕f7 with the initiative.

**25 ♘xa8 ♗g6??**

A horrible mistake. Black can retain slightly better chances with 25...♘c5! 26 ♕c3 ♗d6!, as then 27 ♗a3 ♘a4! 28 ♕b3 ♗xa3 29 ♕xa3 ♖xa8 30 ♘xf5 ♕xf5 31 ♕xa4 ♕g5+ is not an option for White.

**26 ♗h3!**

Now White is winning.

**26...♗c5+ 27 ♔h1 ♗e3 28 ♗xe6 ♕e7 29 ♖f1 ♖xa8**

White has emerged with an extra piece. The end was in line with the rule of exchanging pieces to exploit a material superiority:

**30 ♗f5 ♗f4 31 ♗xg6 hxg6 32 ♗c1 ♖c8 33 ♗xf4 exf4 34 ♘e4 ♕d7 35 ♔g2 b6 36 ♖f2 ♕f5 37 ♖c2 ♖d8 38 ♕c4 g5 39 h3 ♔h7 40 ♖c3 a5 41 a4 1-0**

### Roiz – Grivas
*European blitz Ch, Panormo 2002*

**1 d4 ♘f6 2 c4 g6 3 ♘c3 ♗g7 4 e4 d6 5 ♘f3 0-0 6 ♗e2 e5 7 ♗e3 ♕e7 8 dxe5**

8 d5 is another popular line.

**8...dxe5 9 ♘d5 ♘xd5 10 cxd5 c6 11 0-0**

A more active try is 11 d6!? ♕d7!? 12 h4, as in Avrukh-Grivas, Athens 2003.

**11...cxd5 12 ♕xd5 ♖d8 13 ♕b3 ♘c6** *(D)*

Black has easily equalized. Each side has one weak and one strong square (d4 and d5), but neither of them is immediately exploitable, as both sides use their pieces to control these

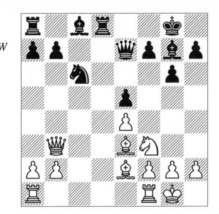

squares. In view of this it is easy to understand why White's next move is mistaken: it weakens d4.

**14 ♗g5? ♗f6! 15 ♗xf6**

White should have admitted the error of his ways and played 15 ♗e3.

**15...♕xf6 16 ♖fd1 ♖xd1+ 17 ♖xd1 ♕e7** *(D)*

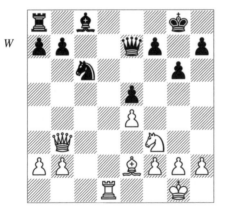

**18 ♗c4?**

A second serious error by White. There was no decent alternative to 18 h3. Admittedly, White also succeeds in planting a minor piece on his own outpost but *the knight cooperates better with its army when occupying an outpost*.

**18...♗g4! 19 h3 ♗xf3**

The tactical sequence 19...♘d4 20 ♗xf7+! ♔g7 21 ♖xd4 exd4 (21...♗xf3 22 ♖a4!) 22 hxg4 ♕xf7 23 ♕d3 would unnecessarily complicate Black's task. After this last exchange Black's game is positionally superior.

**20 ♕xf3 ♘d4 21 ♕d3 ♖c8! 22 ♗d5?!**

It is hard to suggest a move for White that would help improve his position; perhaps 22 ♔h2!?.

**22...♖c2 23 ♖d2??** *(D)*

Black's superiority was becoming more and more obvious, but with the passive 23 ♖b1 White could at least fight on.

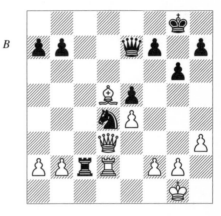

**23...♘f3+!! 0-1**

White resigned in view of 24 gxf3 ♕g5+!. This standard tactical shot was the direct consequence of Black's positional superiority.

### Grivas – A. Vajda
*Budapest 2001*

**1 d4 g6 2 c4 ♗g7 3 e4 d6 4 ♘c3 ♘d7 5 ♘f3 e5 6 ♗e2 ♘gf6 7 0-0 0-0 8 ♕c2 h6?!**

I believe Black should have followed the main line with 8...c6 9 ♖d1 ♖e8.

**9 ♖d1 ♖e8** *(D)*

**10 dxe5!**

White weakens the d4-square but his space advantage, good piece control over d4 and queenside activity more than compensate for this small concession.

**10...dxe5 11 c5! c6 12 b4 ♕c7**

Or 12...a5?! 13 b5! ♕c7 14 bxc6 bxc6 15 ♘a4 with better chances for White.

**13 a3 ♘f8 14 h3! ♘e6 15 ♗e3**

White is fully in control of the 'weak' d4-square. His immediate plans involve the manoeuvre ♘a4-b2-c4-d6, occupying the outpost that has been created in Black's camp.

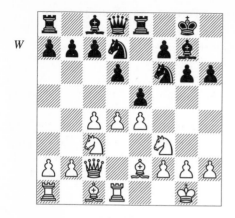

W

**15...♗d7?!**

Black fails to appreciate what will follow. 15...♘h7!? was his only practical chance, intending 16...♘hg5.

**16 ♖d6!!** *(D)*

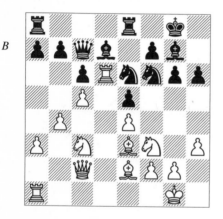

B

The introduction to an exchange sacrifice (through the outpost on d6) that Black is forced to accept.

**16...♗f8**

After 16...♘f8 17 ♖ad1 ♖ad8 18 ♕d2! or 16...♘f4 17 ♗c4! Black's position is about to collapse.

**17 ♖ad1! ♗xd6 18 cxd6 ♕d8 19 ♘xe5 ♖c8 20 ♗c4**

Black is in a tragic state, not knowing what to do with his 'useless' rooks. White calmly prepares his attack on the kingside.

**20...♘h7 21 f4 b5 22 ♗b3 ♖f8 23 ♕f2 ♕f6!?**

Black tries to free himself by returning the material, but even this attempt fails.

**24 ♘xd7 ♕xc3 25 ♗xe6 fxe6 26 ♘xf8 ♘xf8** *(D)*

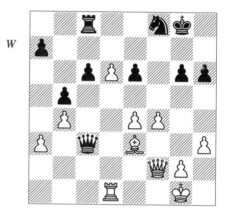

W

Black has gained a respite, but it is only temporary. The weaknesses in his pawn-structure and around his king are too many. Moreover, White has a strong passed pawn and bishop vs knight.

**27 f5! ♕b3 28 ♖f1!**

White now focuses on opening up the position and checkmating the black king.

**28...g5 29 h4! ♕c4 30 hxg5 ♕xe4 31 gxh6 exf5**

Or 31...♕xf5? 32 ♕g3+ ♕g6 33 ♖xf8+!.

**32 ♕g3+ ♔f7**

It would have been much nicer (for White!) if the game had ended with the impressive sequence 32...♕g4 33 ♕xg4+ fxg4 34 ♖xf8+!! ♖xf8 (34...♔xf8 35 ♗d4! ♔g8 36 ♗f6!) 35 ♗g5! ♖f7 36 ♗e7!.

**33 ♕g7+ ♔e6 34 ♕e7+ ♔d5 35 ♖d1+ 1-0**

Overall this was a very original and instructive game, where several strategic elements were employed: outpost, exchange sacrifice, passed pawn, attack on the king. In accordance with the needs of the position, White constantly transformed his superiority from one element to another, without ever losing his advantage.

# Open File

The creation of an open file and its occupation by a rook or even the queen is a strategic element very often encountered.

In the vast majority of games played there occurs an open file, which in most cases 'goes by unnoticed' or simply cannot be exploited by either player. There does exist a third viewpoint of course, which states that many players are at a loss when coming across this very common strategic element and fail to exploit it.

What is the use of an open file anyway? It is effectively a path via which the side that is better placed to do so can penetrate the opponent's camp. This invasion will create threats and interrupt the communication between the opponent's pieces.

Thus, the creation and occupation of an open file greatly increase our chances of achieving our overall aim of winning the game. But what are the specifics, the hidden details if you like, that define the thin line between success and failure? A possible description follows:

1) Selection of the (already or in the near future) open file and evaluation of its significance for furthering our plans.

2) Care so that the open file can be exploited by us and not our opponent. Otherwise our main priority should be to keep the file closed.

3) Transfer of our rooks to the file about to open in advance, so that we are ready to assume its control.

4) Possibility of instant transfer (or at least faster than the opponent) of our rooks to the file already or soon-to-be open.

5) Preservation of our control over the open file by doubling our rooks or avoiding their exchange for the enemy ones.

6) Exploitation of the open file by invading with our rook(s) into the enemy lines, particularly the 7th and 8th ranks.

7) Cooperation of our rook(s) with our remaining pieces to enforce our aims.

The aforementioned essentially constitute the alphabet of the open file concept. Their application in practice is a difficult mission but can be taught; through time and experience there are a lot of benefits to be had.

## Grivas – Hornung
*Munich 1987*

**1 d4 ♘f6 2 c4 c5 3 d5 e5 4 ♘c3 d6 5 e4 ♗e7 6 ♗e2**

The most popular line. One also sees 6 g3!?; e.g., 6...0-0 7 ♗h3 a6 8 ♗xc8 ♕xc8 9 ♕e2 b5 10 cxb5 ± or 6...a6 7 a4 ♘bd7 8 ♗h3 ♖b8 9 ♕c2 b6 10 ♘ge2 ± Ftačnik-Vaisman, Bucharest 1978.

**6...0-0 7 ♘f3 ♘e8** *(D)*

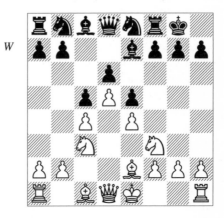

Black's plans revolve around the pawn-breaks ...b5 and ...f5. His last move leans towards the latter option, which also is the easier to achieve.

**8 0-0 ♘d7 9 ♘e1?!**

A more accurate treatment is 9 a3 g6 (9...a6?! 10 b4 b6 11 ♖b1 g6 12 ♗h6 ♘g7 13 ♕d2 ♘f6 14 ♘e1 ♘g4 15 ♗xg4 ♗xg4 16 ♘d3 ♕c7 17 ♖b2 ♗d7 18 f4 with advantage for White, Knaak-Partos, Bucharest 1973) 10 ♗h6 ♘g7

11 ♕d2 ♘f6 12 b4 b6 13 ♘e1 ♔h8 14 bxc5 bxc5 15 f4 exf4 16 ♗xf4 ♘d7 17 ♘d3 ± Malich-Jansa, Havana OL 1966.

**9...♗g5! 10 ♘d3 a6**

This was hardly necessary. 10...g6 is more in the spirit of the position.

**11 a3 g6 12 b4 b6 13 ♖b1**

White prepares to open up and occupy the b-file, thus obtaining a strong initiative on the queenside.

**13...♘g7 14 bxc5 bxc5 15 ♗xg5 ♕xg5 16 ♕c1!** *(D)*

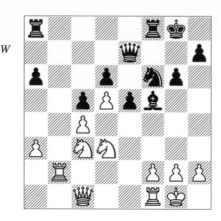

W

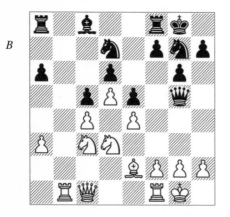

B

With the queens off, Black will be unable to create activity on the kingside to counterbalance White's b-file play.

**16...♕e7! 17 ♖b2!**

Preparing a possible doubling of the rooks on the b-file while, as will become clear in the future, the b2-rook performs some defensive duties as well.

**17...f5 18 exf5**

This was compulsory. Black was threatening ...f4 and ...g5, with good attacking chances.

**18...♘xf5!**

After 18...gxf5 19 f4! e4 20 ♘f2, intending ♘cd1-e3 and later g4!, White has the advantage.

**19 ♗g4 ♘f6!**

19...♘d4?! 20 ♘e4 ♘f6 21 ♘xf6+ ♕xf6 22 ♗xc8 ♖axc8 leads to an ending favourable for White. Black must be very careful in order to preserve the balance.

**20 ♗xf5 ♗xf5** *(D)*

20...gxf5?! 21 f4 leaves White with some advantage.

**21 ♕d2 ♖f7?**

Black had made full use of White's opening inaccuracy and retained, up to this point, a dynamic position with chances for both sides. Now, however, it was time to contest the b-file with 21...♖ab8! 22 ♖fb1 ♕c7, maintaining the balance.

**22 f3! ♖af8 23 ♘f2**

Black's activity has been extinguished, while White is planning ♖e1 and ♘fe4, exchanging down to a promising ending (due to possession of the open b-file).

**23...♗c8 24 ♘fe4 ♘xe4 25 ♘xe4 ♖f4 26 ♖b6**

White's rook has invaded the b-file. White's threats force the black pieces to defensive (and consequently passive) positions.

**26...♖d8 27 ♖e1 ♕f8** *(D)*

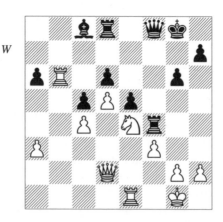

W

White controls the only open file and has already started pressurizing Black's weaknesses;

thus, he has the initiative and the advantage. One standard plan here is the advance of the a-pawn to a5, where it will support the white rook and fix the weak black pawn on a6.

**28 a4! ♗f5**

Black has no better options. The e4-knight is excellently placed and must be exchanged sooner or later.

**29 a5!**

White should not hurry with 29 ♖xa6? ♗xe4 30 ♖xe4 ♖xe4 31 fxe4 ♖b8!, when he has won a pawn (which was doomed anyway) but allowed Black good counterplay.

**29...♗xe4 30 ♖xe4**

Piece exchanges are in White's favour since they reduce Black's possibilities for counter-play while the weaknesses in Black's camp become more accessible.

**30...♖xe4 31 fxe4 ♖a8 32 ♕e3 ♖b8 33 ♕f2!** *(D)*

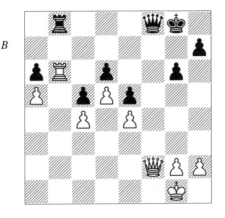

Black cannot exchange his passive rook; this allows White to increase his superiority by tactical means.

**33...♕d8 34 ♕b2! ♖a8**

After 34...♖xb6 35 axb6 White's b-pawn will promote: 35...a5 36 b7 ♕b8 37 ♕b6 a4 38 ♕c6 a3 39 ♕c8+.

**35 g3 ♕f6 36 ♕e2! ♕f8 37 ♔g2 ♕f6 38 ♕f3 ♕d8?!**

Black should have tested White's technique in the rook ending by exchanging the queens, or tried 38...♕g5!?, when White would have to continue with 39 ♕e2! ♕f6 40 ♕g4!.

**39 ♖b7! ♕e8 40 ♕f6 ♖d8? 1-0**

Black resigned before White could play 41 ♕g7#. However, 40...♕f8 41 ♕e6+ ♔h8 42 ♖f7 ♕d8 43 ♖e7! ♕f8 44 ♕xd6 +− is also easy for White.

## Gotsche – Grivas
*Dortmund 1991*

**1 d4 f5 2 e4 fxe4 3 ♘c3 ♘f6 4 f3 ♘c6**

Black chooses to decline the offered pawn, preferring instead to develop harmoniously.

**5 fxe4**

Another possibility is 5 d5 ♘e5 6 fxe4.

**5...e5** *(D)*

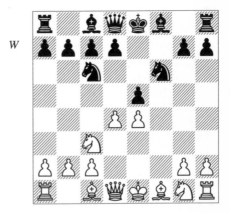

**6 dxe5?!**

Aggressive but not best. White should prefer 6 d5 ♘d4 7 ♘f3 with chances for both sides.

**6...♘xe5 7 ♘f3 ♘xf3+ 8 ♕xf3 ♗b4!**

Black develops methodically, preventing the annoying e5, as now 9 e5?! would be met by 9...♕e7 10 ♗f4 ♗xc3+ 11 bxc3 0-0.

**9 ♗c4 ♕e7! 10 ♗d2 d6 11 h3 ♗e6 12 ♗d3**

Any exchange would favour Black, who already has a clear plan (to exploit the isolated e4-pawn).

**12...0-0 13 ♕e2**

13 0-0-0? is wrong, leading after 13...♗xc3 14 ♗xc3 ♘d5! to the destruction of White's pawn-structure.

**13...♘d7! 14 0-0-0 ♘e5 15 ♔b1 ♗c5**

Preventing the equalizing 16 ♘d5 ♗xd5 17 exd5 ♗xd2 18 ♖xd2.

**16 ♘d5 ♕d7!** *(D)*

**17 ♘e3 ♘xd3!**

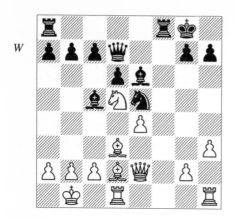

A seemingly irrational exchange of the excellently placed e5-knight for the restricted
d3-bishop. Black simplifies the position by exchanging pieces, obtains the advantage of the
bishop-pair and prepares to launch an attack
(by ...♛a4 and ...♝d4) in case of the inferior
18 cxd3. Thus the e4-pawn is further weakened.

**18 ♛xd3 ♖ae8 19 ♖hf1 ♖xf1 20 ♖xf1 ♛a4!
21 b3 ♛d4!**

Offering another exchange. White must play
with great care so as not to lose material.

**22 ♝c1 ♝f7!**

More black pieces will contribute to the
pressure on e4 (rook on e8, bishop on g6).

**23 ♖f4 ♝g6 24 ♘f5 ♝xf5! 25 ♛xd4 ♝xd4
26 exf5 ♝f6** *(D)*

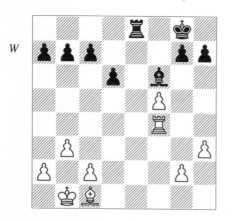

With his last few moves Black exchanged
two clear strategic advantages (two bishops,
isolated e-pawn) for a more decisive one, the

possession of the open e-file, through which he
will invade the enemy lines. The limited material complicates White's defensive task, as he
cannot control all possible entry points (e2, e1).
The position can be considered won for Black.
Such instances of transformations of advantages
are quite common in modern chess. Knowledge
of all strategic elements and its correct application in practice allow for several such operations. Naturally, experience also has its say!

**27 ♖f1 ♖e2 28 g3**

No salvation was offered by 28 g4 ♖h2 29 g5
♝e5 30 f6 gxf6 31 gxf6 ♚f7 32 ♖f3 ♖h1!.

**28...♖h2 29 h4 ♖g2 30 ♝f4 h5!**

Immobilizing the white kingside pawns. The
activation of the black king will prove decisive.

**31 a4 a5 32 ♚c1 ♚f7 33 ♚d1 ♝e5!**

The last detail. White will either lose material or allow Black a passed e-pawn, a much
more active king and possession of the 2nd
rank; these are obvious advantages that suffice
for victory.

**34 ♝xe5 dxe5 35 ♖f3 b6 0-1**

White resigned in view of 36 ♖c3 c5 37 ♖d3
♚f6 38 ♖d6+ ♚f5 39 ♖xb6 ♖xg3 40 ♖b5 g5!
41 hxg5 h4.

### Grivas – R. Simić
*Athens 1991*

1 d4 ♘f6 2 c4 g6 3 ♘c3 d5 4 ♘f3 ♝g7 5 ♝g5
♘e4 6 ♝h4 ♘xc3 7 bxc3 c5 8 cxd5 ♛xd5 9 e3
♘c6 10 ♝e2 cxd4 11 cxd4 b6 12 0-0 ♝b7 13
♛b3! *(D)*

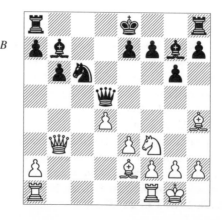

White's best option. His strong centre guarantees a persistent edge in the resulting endgame.

**13...♕xb3 14 axb3 0-0 15 b4! a6**

A new move. White retains a pleasant position after 15...e6 16 b5 ♘a5 17 ♗e7! ♖fc8 18 ♗b4 a6 19 ♗xa5 bxa5 20 ♖xa5 axb5 21 ♖xb5! ♗xf3 22 ♗xf3, when his winning chances amount to approximately 70%, with a 30% drawing margin. Another alternative was the passive but acceptable 15...♖fe8.

**16 ♖ab1 e6 17 ♘d2!**

The threatened 18 ♘c4 (with pressure on b6 and d6) is very dangerous. Black has no choice, since the alternative 17...b5 18 ♘b3! is hardly to his liking.

**17...♘a7 18 ♖fc1! e5!?**

After 18...♖fc8 19 ♘c4! Black faces imminent danger. On the other hand, White now effortlessly gains control of the c-file and the 7th rank.

**19 ♖c7 ♗c6 20 d5!! *(D)***

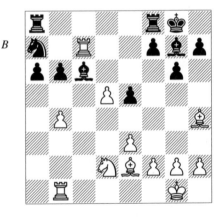

An excellent move, keeping the black pieces passive. The difficulty in choosing this move lies in the fact that a strong central pawn is exchanged for an irrelevant flank one. However, the resulting benefits are clearly significant and thus this is a highly logical move.

**20...♗xd5 21 ♗xa6 ♘c8 22 b5!**

Another difficult move, practically hemming in the a6-bishop, but White is focusing on restricting the black pieces, an aim achieved by difficult moves such as 20 d5!! and 22 b5!.

**22...f6 23 e4 ♗f7 24 f3!**

The h4-bishop is no longer useful on the h4-d8 diagonal and prepares to switch to a new field (g1-a7).

**24...♗h6 25 ♘f1 f5 26 ♖d1 ♗e6 27 ♗f2 fxe4 28 fxe4 ♖f7 29 ♖d8+! ♖f8 30 ♖d3 ♖f7 31 ♖c6!**

White's superiority is decisive. The open c- and d-files are controlled by White, while the black pieces are uncoordinated and lack any potential for improvement.

**31...♗g4 32 ♖d8+ ♖f8 33 ♖xf8+ ♗xf8 34 ♘e3 ♗d7 35 ♖c7 ♗e6 36 ♘d5**

Now Black has to choose between dropping material or surrendering the bishop-pair. In both cases White's superiority will grow significantly.

**36...♗xd5 37 exd5 ♘e7 38 ♖d7 ♖b8 39 g4!! *(D)***

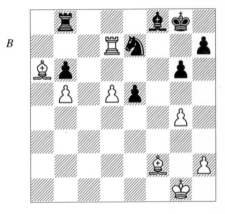

Black has no useful moves (39...h5 40 h3 hxg4 41 hxg4 changes nothing) and will lose material after ♗g3 or ♗b7. White's correct strategy bears fruit.

**39...♔f7 40 d6 1-0**

Black resigned in view of 40...♔e8 41 dxe7 ♔xd7 42 exf8♕ ♖xf8 43 ♗xb6.

### Grivas – K. Karanikolas
*Athens 1996*

**1 d4 d5 2 c4 e6 3 ♘f3 ♘f6 4 ♘c3 ♗e7 5 ♗g5 0-0 6 e3 h6 7 ♗h4 b6 8 ♗d3**

One of White's several options in the popular Tartakower Variation of the Queen's Gambit.

**8...♗b7 9 0-0 ♘bd7 (D)**

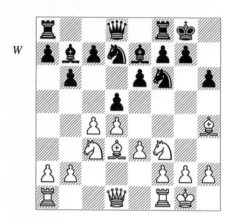

W

**10 cxd5!? ♘xd5?!**

Seeking piece exchanges, but 10...exd5 is preferable.

**11 ♗g3! ♘7f6**

11...♘xc3 12 bxc3 c5 13 e4 is an interesting possibility.

**12 ♘xd5 ♗xd5?!**

As above, 12...exd5 is more in the spirit of the variation. Black is trying to achieve the exchange of the c- and d-pawns, hoping to achieve full equality.

**13 ♕e2 ♘e4**

Black faces problems after 13...c5 14 ♖fd1! cxd4 (14...♗xf3 15 ♕xf3 cxd4 16 ♗a6!) 15 ♘xd4.

**14 ♗e5! ♗d6**

White also has the advantage after 14...f6 15 ♕c2!.

**15 ♖fd1 ♕e7 16 ♖ac1 (D)**

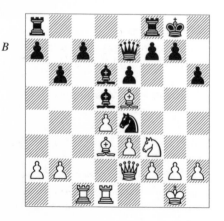

B

Black has failed to achieve the equalizing ...c5 under favourable conditions. His position is now inferior, and becomes even worse after his next move.

**16...f5?! 17 ♗c4!**

White changes tack! He will now fight for the advantage by exploiting the c-file, Black's weakened pawn-structure and the outpost on e5.

**17...♘f6 18 ♗xd5 ♘xd5**

It is too late for 18...exd5, as after 19 ♕d3! ♘e4 20 ♖c6! Black has not brought about any significant changes.

**19 a3 ♘f6 20 ♖c6! ♘d7 21 ♗xd6 cxd6 22 ♖dc1 (D)**

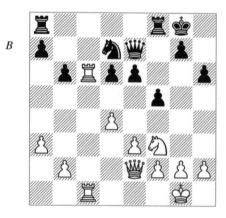

B

White somewhat 'improved' Black's pawn-structure but has fulfilled the important aim of occupying the c-file. The exploitation of this advantage is not difficult but requires concentration and thought.

**22...a6 23 ♕c4!**

Threatening 24 ♕b4 and thus forcing Black to weaken the e5-square.

**23...d5 24 ♕d3 ♖a7 25 g3 ♔h7 26 ♔g2**

White does not hurry and makes some generally useful moves, as Black cannot improve his position.

**26...♖f6 27 ♕c3 b5 28 ♖c7!**

The exchange of the 'good' c7-rook for the 'bad' a7-rook will allow White quicker access to Black's weak queenside pawns.

**28...♖xc7 29 ♕xc7 ♖f7 30 ♕b7! b4 31 ♕xa6 bxa3 32 bxa3**

White has won material and the end is near.

32...e5 33 ♖c7! exd4 34 ♖xd7! ♕xd7 35 ♘e5 ♕e7 36 ♕g6+ 1-0

Black resigned due to 36...♔g8 37 ♕xf7+ ♕xf7 38 ♘xf7 ♔xf7 (38...d3 39 ♔f1; 38...dxe3 39 ♘e5!) 39 exd4.

### Grivas – Koskinen
*Gausdal 1993*

1 d4 d5 2 c4 c6 3 ♘f3 ♘f6 4 e3 e6 5 ♘c3 ♘bd7 6 ♕c2 ♗d6 7 ♗e2 0-0 8 0-0 ♖e8 9 ♖d1 ♕e7 10 b3 b6 11 e4! dxe4 12 ♘xe4 ♘xe4 13 ♕xe4 ♗b7 14 ♗f4! ♗xf4

14...c5 and 14...♖ad8 are other options for Black.

15 ♕xf4 *(D)*

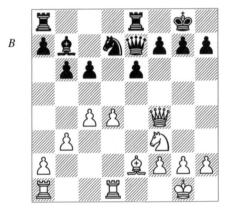

15...e5?!

This liberating attempt fails to solve Black's problems. A better idea is 15...c5 16 ♘e5! with a slight edge for White.

16 ♘xe5!

Black has a satisfactory game after 16 dxe5?! c5!.

16...♘xe5 17 ♕xe5

Again 17 dxe5?! is met by 17...c5!.

17...♕xe5

The only serious option. If 17...♕d7 then 18 ♕h5! g6 19 ♕f3 c5 20 d5.

18 dxe5 ♖xe5

Black is still unable to play the liberating 18...c5?: 19 f4 f6 20 ♖d7! ♖ab8 (20...♗c8 21 ♖c7 fxe5 22 fxe5 ♖xe5 23 ♗f3) 21 ♗h5! g6 22 exf6!.

19 ♗f3 ♖ae8 *(D)*

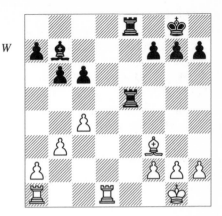

An original and interesting position. Each side controls an open file. However, the d-file is more vulnerable as the entry points on it (d6, d7 and d8) cannot be controlled as efficiently as those on the e-file (e3, e2 and e1). Moreover, the white king is closer to the entry point e1 than its black counterpart is to d8. Finally, the correlation of the two bishops and the c6-pawn is also of significance. Overall, White is better.

20 h3 ♔f8

White would remain superior after 20...♖5e7 21 c5! or 20...♗a8 21 ♖d7 ♖5e7 22 ♖ad1.

21 b4! ♖5e7 22 c5 ♖e5 23 ♖ac1 bxc5 24 bxc5 ♔e7 25 ♖d4!

Intending to attack Black's weaknesses (a7 and c6). The e-file has proven worthless for Black, while White now also abandons his file, adapting to the changed circumstances.

25...♖d8 26 ♖a4 a6 27 ♖b4 ♖d7 28 ♖c2! *(D)*

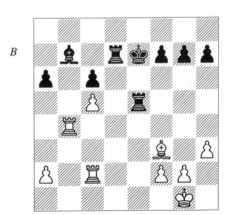

Protecting the 2nd rank and at the same time threatening a future ♗e2, winning the a6-pawn.

**28...♖c7 29 ♖b6 ♖e1+ 30 ♔h2 ♖e5 31 ♗e2 a5 32 ♗a6!**

The exchange of bishops will further highlight Black's weak pawns. He is now unable to avoid material losses.

**32...♗c8 33 ♗xc8 ♖xc8 34 ♖a6 ♔e6 35 ♖xa5**

From now on the game is not of interest (as regards our subject). White won material and carefully converted this into victory in the ensuing rook ending:

**35...♖c7 36 ♖a8 ♖d5 37 ♖e8+ ♔f6 38 ♖a8 ♔e6 39 ♖a6 ♖dd7 40 ♖b6 ♔d5 41 ♖b3 ♖a7 42 ♖e3 ♖dc7 43 ♖d3+ ♔e4 44 ♖d6 f6 45 ♖c4+ ♔f5 46 a4 ♖a6 47 g4+ ♔g6 48 h4 h6 49 ♔g3 ♖e7 50 h5+ ♔f7 51 ♔f4 ♖e5 52 ♖d7+ ♔f8 53 ♖c7 ♖e7 54 ♖xe7 ♔xe7 55 ♔f5 ♖a7 56 f4 ♔f7 57 ♖d4 ♔e7 58 ♔g6 ♔e8 59 a5 ♔f8 60 ♖a4 ♖a6 61 ♖a2 ♔g8 62 ♖b2 ♔f8 63 ♖b7 ♖xa5 64 ♖xg7 ♖xc5 65 ♖f7+ ♔e8 66 ♖xf6 1-0**

### Likavsky – Grivas
*Iraklion 1997*

**1 d4 ♘f6 2 c4 g6 3 ♘c3 ♗g7 4 e4 d6 5 ♘f3 0-0 6 ♗e2 e5 7 0-0 ♘bd7 8 ♕c2 c6 9 ♖d1 ♕e7 10 ♖b1 a5 11 b3 ♖e8**

White was slightly better after 11...♘h5 12 g3 ♖e8 13 d5 in Lautier-Hort, Novi Sad OL 1990. Another decent possibility at Black's disposal is 11...exd4 12 ♘xd4 ♘c5 13 f3 ♘h5! 14 g4 ♘f6 15 ♗f4 ♘fd7 16 ♗g3 ♘e5 17 ♕d2 ♖d8 with unclear play, Schmidt-Knaak, Dresden 1985.

**12 d5 ♘c5 13 ♗e3!? (D)**

**13...a4!!**

After the mistaken 13...♘cxe4? 14 ♘xe4 ♘xe4 15 ♕xe4 ♗f5 16 ♕h4 ♕xh4 17 ♘xh4 ♗xb1 18 ♖xb1 cxd5 19 cxd5 ♖ec8 20 a4!! and 21 ♗c4 the black rooks lack a promising field of action due to the shortage of open files. Thus, White's minor pieces will be able to regroup any way and any time.

**14 b4?**

A mechanical and ultimately mistaken reaction. White should have opted for 14 ♘d2 (14 ♗xc5? axb3! 15 axb3 dxc5 gives the advantage

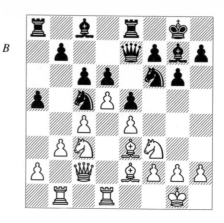

to Black, who has the clear plan ...♘e8-d6) 14...axb3 15 axb3 with chances for both sides.

**14...♘cxe4! 15 ♘xe4 ♘xe4 16 ♕xe4 ♗f5 17 ♕h4 ♕xh4 18 ♘xh4 ♗xb1 19 ♖xb1 cxd5 20 cxd5 ♖ec8 (D)**

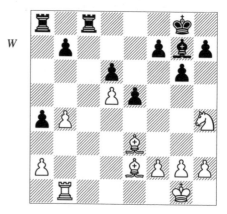

The difference between this and 13...♘cxe4? is visible: Black's rooks are active along the c-file, while the white pieces lack the time necessary to regroup and establish coordination.

**21 ♗d1 ♖c3! 22 ♘f3 ♖a3! 23 ♖b2 e4 24 ♘d4 ♖d3! 25 ♗e2 ♗xd4 26 ♗xd3 ♗xb2**

Black has increased his material gains. Overall, only one (but very serious) error was necessary on White's part (14 b4?). The open c-file proved to be of decisive importance, and the way Black managed to keep it open and exploit it was very instructive.

**27 ♗xe4 ♖c8 28 b5 ♗d4 29 ♗f4 f5 30 ♗d3 ♖c3 31 ♗b1 ♖c5 32 ♗d3 ♔g7 33 ♔f1 ♖xd5 34 ♔e2 ♗xf2 35 ♗c2 ♗b6 0-1**

## Grivas – Nunn

*Match (game 2), Athens 1991*

**1 d4 ♘f6 2 c4 g6 3 ♘c3 ♗g7 4 e4 d6 5 h3 ♘bd7 6 ♗e3 e5 7 d5 ♘c5 8 ♕c2 0-0 9 g4 c6 10 ♘ge2**

After the careless 10 b4?! cxd5! 11 cxd5 ♘cxe4! 12 ♘xe4 ♘xe4 13 ♕xe4 f5! Black would enjoy a strong initiative for the piece.

**10...cxd5 11 cxd5 ♗d7 12 ♘g3 ♖c8 13 g5!?** *(D)*

A new move. White had previously preferred the unclear 13 ♕d2.

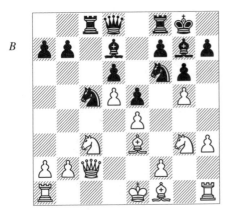

**13...♘h5?!**

Black should prefer 13...♘e8!? 14 ♕d2 f5 15 gxf6 ♘xf6 16 ♖b1 ±.

**14 ♘xh5 gxh5 15 ♕d2**

15 ♗e2?! b5! allows Black some initiative and is therefore inferior.

**15...♕a5! 16 ♖b1 ♕b4!**

The only move. Not 16...♘a4? 17 ♘b5!.

**17 a3 ♕b3 18 ♗e2 f5!**

Black proceeds actively, fighting for his share of the play. The passive 18...h4? 19 ♗g4! would only lead to trouble.

**19 gxf6 ♖xf6 20 ♗xh5 ♘a4?**

This is a serious mistake. Black should play 20...♕c4! 21 ♗e2 ♘xe4 22 ♕c2 ♕a2!! 23 ♕xe4 ♖xc3 24 bxc3 ♗f5 25 ♕b4 ♕xb1+ 26 ♕xb1 ♗xb1 27 c4 with only a slight advantage for White.

**21 ♗d1! ♕c4 22 ♗e2 ♕b3 23 ♘xa4 ♕xa4**

23...♗xa4 24 ♖c1! would not help.

**24 ♗d3! ♖f3 25 ♖g1 ♔h8** *(D)*

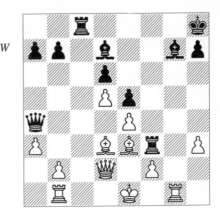

**26 ♖c1**

26 h4 was also not bad, but White realizes that occupation of the c-file is more significant. His only problem is the placement of his king, while possible major-piece exchanges would clearly favour him in the resulting ending.

**26...♖xh3 27 ♖xc8+ ♗xc8 28 ♕c3! ♕d7 29 ♔d2!!**

Clearing the g1-rook's path to the c-file. Black's hand is forced.

**29...♕d8 30 ♖c1! ♗g4 31 ♕c7! ♗f6 32 ♗e2!**

Another significant exchange, allowing all the remaining white pieces to become more active than their black counterparts.

**32...♕xc7 33 ♖xc7 ♗xe2 34 ♔xe2 h5 35 ♖xb7**

White's material gain weighs heavily now, as Black has no counterplay.

**35...♖h1 36 ♔f3**

36 ♖f7! would win more easily. White must keep an eye on the passed black h-pawn.

**36...♖g1! 37 ♖c7 ♗g5 38 ♗xg5 ♖xg5 39 ♖f7! ♖g1 40 ♖f5 ♔g7 41 ♖xh5 ♖b1** *(D)*

The execution of favourable exchanges (also via the c-file) and the exploitation of the open file have brought White to a winning rook ending. Naturally, some care and good ideas are still required.

**42 ♔g4! ♔g6**

Or 42...♖xb2 43 ♔f5 ♖xf2+ 44 ♔e6 ♖f4 (44...♖f6+ 45 ♔e7 ♖g6 46 ♖f5 ♖h6 47 ♖f7+) 45 ♔xd6 ♖xe4 46 ♖xe5 ♖a4 47 ♖e3.

**43 ♖h8 ♖xb2 44 f4!**

The last difficult move.

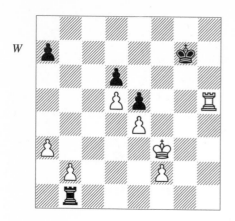

44...Rg2+ 45 Kf3 Ra2 46 fxe5 dxe5 47 Re8 Rxa3+ 48 Kg4 Ra6 49 Rxe5 Kf7 50 Rh5 Rg6+ 51 Kf5 1-0

### Grivas – P. Pandavos
*Athens 1987*

1 d4 Nf6 2 Nf3 d5 3 c4 e6 4 Nc3 Be7 5 Bg5 h6 6 Bh4 0-0 7 e3 Nbd7

When Black has already played ...h6, the Tartakower Variation (7...b6) represents a better choice.

8 Rc1 c6 9 a3 dxc4

Black could also try 9...a6!? but he has decided to exchange some pieces to free his restricted position.

10 Bxc4 Nd5 (D)

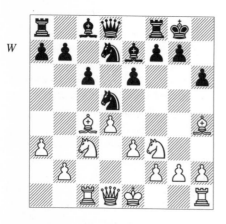

11 Bg3!

Without the interpolation of 5...h6 6 Bh4 White would now have to exchange the dark-squared bishops, thus further relieving Black's congestion.

11...Nxc3 12 Rxc3 c5?

Opening the position can hardly favour Black, who is behind in development. Instead, he should have tried 12...b5!? 13 Bd3 b4 14 Rxc6 bxa3 15 bxa3 Bxa3 16 0-0 ±.

13 0-0 cxd4 14 Nxd4 Nb6 15 Bb3

White is much better, as Black is unable to complete his development (15...Bd7 16 Wf3!) while his pieces remain scattered, without any targets or counterplay.

15...Nd5 16 Rc2 Bd6!? 17 Bxd6 Wxd6 18 Nf3!

By threatening 19 e4 White forces Black into an unpleasant endgame with an isolated black pawn and White controlling the important open c-file.

18...Wd8 19 Bxd5

19 Rd2 Wf6! was just a mirage.

19...exd5 20 Wd4! Be6 21 Rfc1 (D)

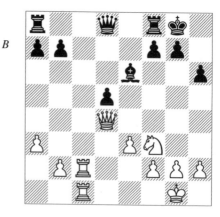

White possesses a host of slight advantages, such as the possession of the c-file, the isolated black d-pawn, the more active queen and a good knight vs a bad bishop. Black's greatest problem is the total lack of active possibilities, forcing him to remain passive and await White's actions. Such positions must be avoided because they lead, slowly but steadily, to defeat.

21...Re8 22 Wb4 Re7 23 Nd4 Rd7 24 Rc3 Wf8

The queen exchange is only superficially favourable for Black. The white king is now able to contribute to the efforts of his army.

**25 ♕xf8+ ♔xf8 26 ♔f1 ♔e7 27 ♔e2 ♔d8 28 h3 h5?!**

Placing the pawns on the same colour square as the bishop cannot be the correct way to defend. Black should have continued 28...♔e7 and 29...f6.

**29 f4! g6 30 ♔f3 ♖e7 31 g4 ♗d7 32 ♖g1 hxg4+ 33 hxg4 ♖c8 34 ♖xc8+ ♗xc8 35 g5** *(D)*

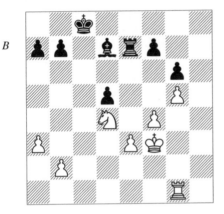

White gave up the c-file as new possibilities have emerged, most notably along the h-file; through this avenue White can penetrate into Black's camp. The recent exchanges have troubled Black even more, as it now proves impossible to defend all his weaknesses. However, was there any choice?

**35...♗f5?**

A decisive error. Black should have stayed passive with 35...♔c7 and ...♔d6 and hoped for mistakes on White's part.

**36 ♘xf5! gxf5 37 ♖d1! ♖d7 38 ♔e2!** *(D)*

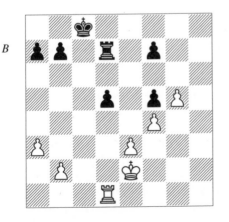

Now the white king will occupy the excellent d4-square, allowing the rook to attack Black's weak pawns.

**38...♔c7 39 ♔d3 ♔d6 40 ♖h1! ♔c5 41 ♖h7 ♔c6 42 ♖h6+ ♖d6**

White was easily winning anyway, because 42...♔c5 43 ♖f6 would not avert the loss of material.

**43 ♔d4! ♔c7 44 ♔e5 ♖d7 45 ♔xf5 ♖e7 46 ♖h3 ♔d6 47 ♔f6 b5 48 f5 1-0**

### Yrjölä – Grivas
*Olympiad, Thessaloniki 1984*

**1 d4 ♘f6 2 c4 g6 3 ♘c3 ♗g7 4 e4 d6 5 ♗e2 0-0 6 ♘f3 e5 7 0-0 ♘c6 8 d5 ♘e7 9 b4 ♘h5 10 c5** *(D)*

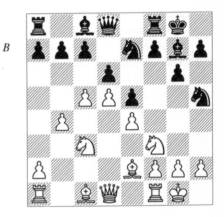

**10...♘f4 11 ♗xf4 exf4 12 ♖c1**

White quickly obtains control of the open c-file but Black now gains decent counterplay, particularly on the semi-open a-file.

**12...a5! 13 ♘b5 axb4 14 cxd6 cxd6 15 ♕b3**

A new move. 15 ♕d2 is more common, but has failed to trouble Black.

**15...♗g4!**

Black completes his development and plans to eliminate the f3-knight.

**16 ♖c7!?** *(D)*

**16...♖e8?**

However, this move is a serious mistake. 16...f5?! is also unsatisfactory. Black's only real problem is the bad placement of the e7-knight. In the game Grivas-Murey, Tel-Aviv 1991, Black (at least) solved this problem after

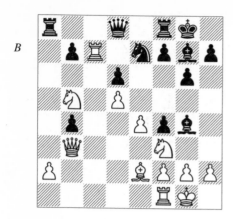

16...♘c8! 17 ♖xb7 ♕a5! 18 ♗c4 ♘b6 19 ♖c7 ♘xc4 20 ♕xc4 ♖fc8 21 ♖c6 ♖xc6 22 ♕xc6 ♕xa2 23 ♘xd6 ♕a7 24 ♘b5 ♕a6 25 ♘fd4 ♗xd4 26 ♕xa6 ♗xf2+ 27 ♖xf2 ♖xa6 28 ♖b2 f3 29 ♘d4 ♖a1+ 30 ♔f2 fxg2 31 ♔xg2 ♖e1 32 ♖xb4 ♖xe4 33 ♖b8+ ♔g7 34 ♘c6 ♗d7 35 ♖b7 ♗xc6 36 dxc6 ♖c4 37 c7 ♔f6 38 ♔f3 ♔e6 39 ♖a7 h5 40 ♔g3 g5 41 ♖b7 f6 42 ♖a7 ♔f5 43 ♖a5+ ♔g6 44 ♖a7 ♖c3+ 45 ♔g2 ♖c2+ 46 ♔g3 h4+ 47 ♔f3 ♔f5 48 h3 ♖c3+ 49 ♔g2 ♔g6 50 ♖b7 ♔h5 51 ♖b6 ♖c2+ 52 ♔g1 ♔g6 53 ♖b7 ½-½.

**17 ♖fc1 ♘f5**

17...f5?! is again unsatisfactory: 18 e5!? (or 18 ♘fd4!?, targeting Black's weakness on e6) 18...♗xe5 (18...♗xf3 19 exd6!) 19 ♘xe5 ♗xe2 20 ♖d7! ♗xb5 (20...♕b6 21 ♘xd6!) 21 ♖xd8 ♖axd8 22 ♕xb4 dxe5 23 ♕xb5 ♘xd5 24 ♖d1 with advantage for White.

**18 ♕xb4! ♖xa2 19 exf5 ♖axe2 20 fxg6 hxg6 21 ♕xf4** *(D)*

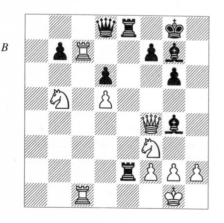

**21...♗d7?**

Black's last error. He had to continue with 21...♗f5! 22 h3 (22 ♖xb7 ♗e5 23 ♕c4; 22 ♕xd6 ♗d3!) 22...♗e5 23 ♘xe5 ♖2xe5! 24 ♖xb7 (24 g4?! ♖xd5! 25 ♖xb7 ♗e4!) 24...♖xd5 25 ♘c7 ♖e4 26 ♘xd5 ♖xf4 27 ♘xf4 ±.

**22 ♘xd6! ♕xc7**

Desperation. Possession of the c-file (initially) and the 7th rank proved too much for Black, who failed to react appropriately.

**23 ♕xf7+ ♔h7 24 ♕xg7+! ♔xg7 25 ♘xe8+ ♗xe8 26 ♖xc7+ ♔f6 27 ♖xb7 ♖a2 28 h4 1-0**

## Soylu – Grivas
*European rapid Ch, Panormo 2002*

**1 e4 c5 2 ♘f3 ♘c6 3 ♗b5 d6 4 ♗xc6+ bxc6 5 0-0 ♗g4**

5...♘f6 is more usual. Black plays too ambitiously.

**6 c3 ♘f6 7 ♖e1 ♘d7 8 d4 e6 9 ♗e3 cxd4 10 cxd4 ♗e7 11 ♘bd2** *(D)*

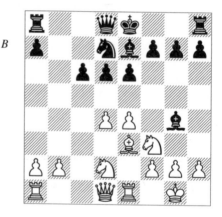

**11...d5?!**

This is inaccurate. Black should have opted for 11...0-0 12 ♖c1 c5 13 dxc5 ±.

**12 ♕a4! ♗xf3**

A compulsory exchange. 12...♕b6? loses immediately to 13 exd5 exd5 14 ♘e5! ♘xe5?? 15 dxe5.

**13 ♘xf3 ♕b6 14 ♘e5 ♘xe5 15 dxe5 ♕b7 16 exd5 exd5 17 ♖ac1 ♖c8!**

Black will lose a pawn anyway, and he correctly chooses to give up the flank a-pawn rather than the more important central c-pawn.

**18 ♕xa7?!**

It is hard to criticize a move that wins a pawn without any risk but I believe that 18 ♖c2! 0-0 19 ♖ec1 is more dangerous for Black.

**18...♕xa7 19 ♗xa7 ♖a8 20 ♗d4**

White could lead the game to a draw here with 20 ♗c5 ♖xa2 21 ♗xe7 ♔xe7 22 ♖xc6 but this decision, taking into account the extra pawn, is very difficult to make and feels 'unjust'.

**20...♔d7 21 a3 ♖hb8** *(D)*

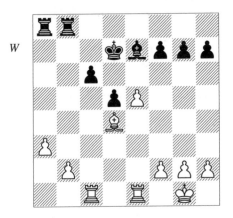

White's extra pawn is not very relevant in this position. Black has compensation down the semi-open a- and b-files, while he can make use of his c- and d-pawns and his more active king.

**22 g3?**

White must proceed carefully and never allow ...c5. Therefore he should continue with 22 ♖e3! and 23 b4!.

**22...♖b5! 23 ♖c2 c5 24 ♗e3 ♔e6**

Black is now better, as his central pawns prove much more mobile than White's flank soldiers. White did not register the change in the position or did not wish to accept this turn of events. Had he done so, then he could have searched for ways to ease the pressure, such as 25 b4!? cxb4 26 axb4, with just a slight edge for Black.

**25 f4 h5! 26 h3 d4! 27 ♗c1 ♖b3! 28 ♔g2 g6 29 ♖f1 ♖ab8** *(D)*

**30 g4?!**

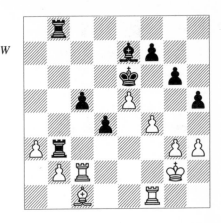

*Opening the h-file is a mistake on White's part, as only Black will be able to exploit it.* In the end this turns out to be the decisive mistake!

**30...hxg4 31 hxg4 ♖h8 32 f5+**

Desperation. White cannot find any satisfactory way to proceed and any rook exchange will allow Black to make progress with ...♔d5 and ...c4, winning quickly. Black's superiority is now obvious and victory is near.

**32...gxf5 33 gxf5+ ♔xe5 34 ♖e2+ ♔f6 35 ♗f4 ♖g8+ 36 ♔h2 ♖g4 37 ♗e5+ ♔g5 38 f6 ♗f8** *(D)*

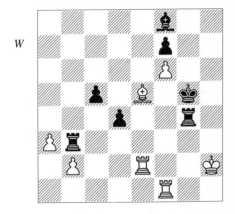

**39 ♖g1?!**

The rook exchange helps Black.

**39...♖xg1 40 ♔xg1 ♔f5 41 ♗c7 d3 42 ♖f2+ ♔e4 43 a4 c4 44 ♔f1 ♗h6 45 a5 ♗e3 46 ♖h2 c3 47 ♖h4+ ♔d5 48 bxc3 ♖b1+ 49 ♔g2 d2 0-1**

# Semi-Open File

A file is semi-open when one of the two sides does not have a pawn on it. This element is closely related to that of the open file, although the differences between them are anything but negligible.

The aims pursued by the exploitation of a semi-open file are multiple, the most important being:

1) Application of pressure on the opponent's pawn on the semi-open file, when this pawn is backward.

2) Forcing the opponent's pieces to defend this pawn, when it is backward.

3) Development of the initiative through the semi-open file.

4) Transformation of the semi-open file to an open one, and exploitation of the open file.

The value of the semi-open file increases when there is a backward pawn on it, as well as outposts.

### Arlandi – Grivas
*European Junior Ch, Groningen 1985/6*

**1 d4 ♘f6 2 c4 g6 3 ♘c3 ♗g7 4 e4 0-0 5 ♘f3 d6 6 ♗e3 c5 7 d5 e6 8 h3 exd5 9 exd5 ♖e8 10 ♗d3 ♗h6** *(D)*

Black gains an outpost on e5 (soon to be created) while White obtains active play down the semi-open f-file. Alternatives include 10...♘bd7 and 10...♘h5, with good chances of equalizing.

**11 0-0 ♗xe3 12 fxe3 ♘bd7**

After 12...♖xe3? 13 ♕d2 ♖e8 14 ♕h6 White has a very strong attack.

**13 e4 ♔g7!**

A new move. 13...♖f8 seems inferior. Black must defend on the semi-open f-file, so he must place his pieces harmoniously, aiming to strengthen his defensive shield and at the same time trying to make use of the outpost on e5. Finally, he can possibly seek activity on the queenside.

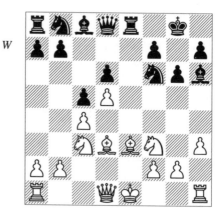

W

**14 ♖f2! ♖e7! 15 ♕d2 ♘e8 16 ♖af1 a6!**

After some preliminary defensive regrouping, Black tries to create counterplay on the queenside. Now the 'natural' reply 17 a4?! would severely weaken White's dark squares on this flank.

**17 ♗c2!**

Threatening 18 ♗a4 and ♗xd7, exchanging the passive white bishop for the black knight that controls the e5-square. Black must react.

**17...b5! 18 cxb5 axb5 19 ♘xb5 ♗a6!**

The black rook is trapped after the tempting 19...♖xa2? 20 ♘a3!.

**20 a4 ♗xb5 21 axb5** *(D)*

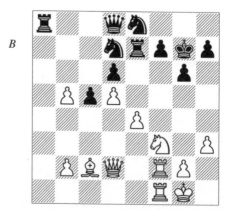

B

**21...♕a5?**

Black gets carried away on the queenside, ignoring the looming dangers on the other flank. 21...♖a7! followed by 22...♘e5 had to be played, when Black would have excellent compensation for the pawn (control over the dark squares, outpost on e5) in an unclear position with chances for both sides.

**22 ♕f4! ♖a7?**

22...♕xb5? 23 ♕h4 ♘df6 24 ♘g5 was just as bad, but Black had to play 22...f6.

**23 ♘g5! ♘df6**

Forced (23...♘e5? 24 ♘e6+! ♔g8 25 ♕h6! ♘d7 26 e5!!).

**24 ♕h4**

White's attack is becoming very dangerous, as now the combinative 25 ♖xf6! ♘xf6 26 ♖xf6 ♔xf6 27 ♘e6+ is threatened.

**24...h6 (D)**

24...♖e5 also offers no salvation: 25 ♖xf6! ♘xf6 26 ♘e6+ ♖xe6 (26...fxe6 27 ♕xf6+ ♔h6 28 ♕f8+ ♔g5 {28...♖g7 29 ♖f7} 29 h4+ ♔xh4 30 ♕f4+ ♔h5 31 ♗d1#) 27 dxe6 ♕d8 28 exf7 ♖xf7 29 g4!.

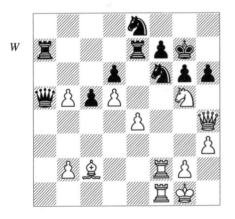

White could now win with 25 ♘e6+! fxe6 26 e5!! (but not 26 ♖xf6? ♘xf6 27 ♕xf6+ ♔h7 28 e5 ♖g7 29 dxe6 ♕d2!), but the game continuation is also very strong.

**25 e5!**

White's last piece joins the attack.

**25...hxg5**

Black cannot play any of the following lines: 25...♖xe5 26 ♘e6+! fxe6 27 ♖xf6; 25...dxe5 26 ♘e6+!; 25...♘xd5 26 ♘xf7! ♖xf7 27 ♕e4

♖xf2 28 ♕xg6+; 25...♘h7 26 ♘xh7 ♔xh7 27 ♕g4!; 25...♘g8 26 ♘e6+! fxe6 (26...♔h8 27 exd6) 27 ♕e4.

**26 exf6+ ♘xf6 27 ♕xg5 ♘e4?!**

The passive 27...♘e8 should have been played, although White retains a very strong attack after 28 h4! intending h5.

**28 ♗xe4 ♖xe4 29 ♕f6+ ♔g8 30 ♕xd6 (D)**

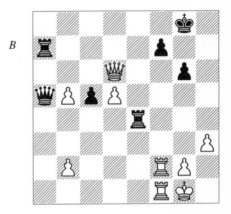

**30...♕c7**

No defence was offered by 30...♕xb5 31 ♖xf7! ♖xf7 32 ♕xg6+ ♖g7 33 ♕xe4.

**31 ♕c6 ♕xc6 32 dxc6 ♖b4 33 ♖xf7!**

The last strike, and it comes via the semi-open f-file! The white c-pawn reaches the promotion square.

**33...♖xf7 34 ♖xf7 1-0**

## Stoica – Grivas
*Sofia 1986*

**1 e4 e5 2 ♗c4 ♘f6 3 d3 ♗e7 4 ♘f3 ♘c6 5 0-0 0-0 6 ♖e1 d6 7 a3!?**

7 ♗b3 is seen more often.

**7...♗e6 8 ♘bd2 ♕d7 9 ♘f1 (D)**

**9...♘d4**

After 9...♗xc4?!, 10 dxc4 (intending ♘e3-d5) would offer White a slight but permanent space advantage.

**10 c3 ♘xf3+ 11 ♕xf3 b5?!**

Offering White a future target. 11...c6 was preferable, with equality.

**12 ♗a2!**

Black would obtain play on the semi-open f-file after 12 ♗xe6?! fxe6.

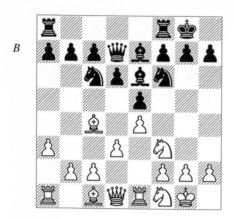

**12...♗xa2 13 ♖xa2 ♕e6 14 ♖a1 ♕g4?!**

A better option was 14...a5!? 15 ♘e3 ♘d7 with equal chances.

**15 ♕e3?!**

White returns the favour. After 15 ♕xg4 ♘xg4 16 a4! he would have the initiative on the queenside.

**15...♘h5! 16 h3 ♕g6 17 ♕f3 ♗g5!**

The exchange of dark-squared bishops helps Black.

**18 ♗xg5 ♕xg5 19 ♘e3 ♘f4 20 ♖ad1 ♕f6 21 ♔h2 ♕e6 22 d4 a6?!**

Black should have supported the e5-square immediately with 22...f6!, in order to keep the d-file closed.

**23 ♖d2?!** *(D)*

White would have the advantage after 23 dxe5 dxe5 24 ♘d5!.

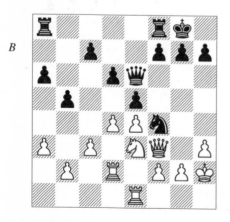

**23...f6! 24 d5 ♕d7 25 ♕g4!? ♕xg4 26 hxg4 ♖fb8!**

Now both sides focus on the queenside. The semi-open h-file is of no real value.

**27 ♖c1 ♖a7 28 g3 ♘g6 29 c4 bxc4?**

29...b4! is more in the spirit of the position; Black then stands well (30 a4 b3!). White can now create threats, making good use of the semi-open c-file, in contrast to Black's harmless play on the b-file. These are the consequences of the careless advance 11...b5?! and Black's superficial treatment of the position.

**30 ♖xc4 ♔f7 31 ♖dc2 ♖bb7 32 ♖a4! ♘e7 33 ♘c4 ♔e8 34 ♘a5 ♖b5 35 b4!** *(D)*

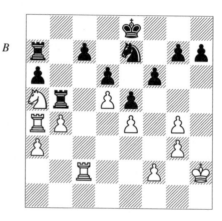

The black pieces have been driven to defensive, passive positions, while White increases his queenside pressure.

**35...♔d7 36 f4 ♖a8 37 f5?**

Too hasty and inappropriate. White will need a breakthrough on some other part of the board, and that can only be the kingside. The possibility of enforcing this breakthrough with a future g5 should have been retained. Black can now defend.

**37...♖bb8 38 ♔g2 ♖b5 39 ♔f3 h6 40 ♔e3** *(D)*

White retains good possibilities to outplay Black, thanks to the weaknesses in his camp (pawns on a6 and c7) and the possession of the semi-open c-file. Black has to be very careful and this would have been best achieved by 40...♖a7 or 40...♖b6.

**40...♖bb8? 41 ♘c6! ♘xc6 42 ♖xc6 a5**

Unfortunately, there is no longer any hope for salvation. Black would also lose after 42...♖b6 43 ♖xb6 cxb6 44 b5! ♔c7 (44...a5 45 ♖c4! ♖c8

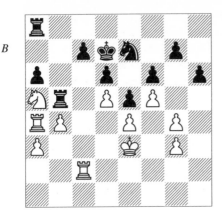

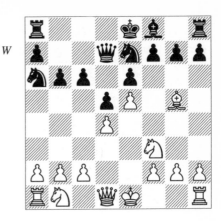

46 Rc6!) 45 ♔f3! ♔b7 46 g5!! hxg5 47 bxa6+ Rxa6 48 Rxa6 ♔xa6 49 ♔g4 ♔a5 50 ♔h5 ♔a4 51 ♔g6 ♔xa3 52 ♔xg7 b5 53 ♔xf6 b4 54 ♔e6 b3 55 f6 b2 56 f7 b1♕ 57 f8♕ ♕xe4 58 ♕xd6+.

**43 bxa5 Rb3+ 44 ♔f2 Ra7 45 a6 ♔c8 46 ♔g2!**

Planning ♔h3-h4-h5-g6. Black can no longer develop any counterplay in order to disturb White's plans. The position is lost.

**46...Rb6 47 ♔h3 Rb3 48 ♔h4 Re3 49 Rac4 Rxa3 50 Rxd6 R7xa6 51 Rxa6 Rxa6 52 ♔h5 ♔d7 53 ♔g6 Ra3 54 ♔xg7 Rxg3 55 ♔xf6 Rxg4 56 ♔xe5 h5 57 Rc6 1-0**

## Bousios – Grivas
*Athens 1987*

**1 d4 e6 2 e4 d5 3 e5 b6**

An old line angling for a quick exchange of the light-squared bishop, which is considered the main problem piece for Black in the French Defence.

**4 ♘f3?!**

A mechanical treatment of the opening. Better is 4 ♗b5+ c6 5 ♗a4 ♗a6 6 ♘e2, intending c3 and ♗c2, or 4 c3 ♕d7 5 f4.

**4...♘e7 5 ♗b5+ c6 6 ♗d3**

Now after 6 ♗a4 ♗a6 White cannot castle.

**6...♗a6 7 ♗xa6 ♘xa6 8 ♗g5 ♕d7 (D)**

Black has solved all his problems and now sets about developing play on the queenside. White, lacking the light-squared bishop, cannot present any serious dangers on the kingside, where he traditionally is superior.

**9 ♕e2 ♘c7 10 ♗xe7?!**

There was no need for this exchange. 10 0-0 was better.

**10...♗xe7 11 0-0 0-0 12 c3 c5**

Black has a firm hold on the initiative. White is condemned to observing events, without the possibility of interfering. Naturally, White's position is by no means lost; he has no significant weaknesses. Defending such a position in practice, however, is a difficult task requiring constant vigilance and tough defence.

**13 ♘bd2 a5 14 Rab1 a4?!**

Somewhat hasty. 14...c4, followed by ...b5-b4, was better.

**15 a3 ♘b5 (D)**

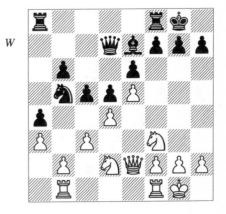

**16 ♕e3**

White must be prepared to support the d4-square with pieces, so as to keep the c-file closed.

**16...Rfc8 17 ♔h1 Ra7 18 Rg1**

Lacking a decent plan, White simply waits for Black to determine events.

**18...cxd4 19 ♘xd4 ♘xd4 20 ♕xd4 ♕b5**

Black will now try to invade White's ranks by making use of the semi-open c-file; it will then be possible to target White's pawns on b2 and e5.

**21 ♘f3 ♖ac7 22 ♖ge1 ♗c5 23 ♕d2 h6 24 ♖bd1 ♖d8 25 ♕e2 ♕b3 26 ♖d2 ♖dc8 27 ♘d4?**

White should have stayed put. The exchange of the remaining minor pieces greatly benefits Black, who is now free to act.

**27...♗xd4 28 ♖xd4 ♖c4 29 ♖ed1 b5** *(D)*

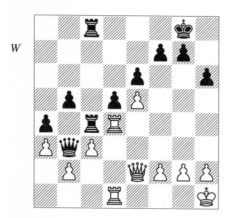

If the black a-pawn were still on a5, Black would easily win with the help of the break ...b4; this would lead to the creation of a very weak white pawn on either b2 or c3. Now, however, things are much more difficult for Black, who retains his advantage but does not have a way to break through.

**30 h3 ♕a2! 31 ♖xc4**

Preventing 31...♖xc3!. 31 ♖1d2 ♖xd4 would not help much, as White must either surrender the c-file (32 cxd4) or weaken his pawn-structure (32 ♖xd4 ♖xc3 33 ♕xb5 ♖c8).

**31...♖xc4 32 f3?!**

The threat was 32...♖e4. White should have transposed to the previous comment with 32 ♖d4.

**32...♖xc3 33 ♕xb5 ♕b3! 34 ♕xb3?**

In the rook ending Black will be clearly better, as he will practically enjoy an extra pawn (the black a4-pawn blocks the white a3- and

b2-pawns). In view of this White should not have acquiesced to the queen exchange and tried 34 ♕e8+ ♔h7 35 bxc3 ♕xd1+ 36 ♔h2 ♔g6! instead, with Black retaining the advantage but White having some practical chances of survival.

**34...♖xb3 35 ♖d2 f6!**

Black's central passed pawns seal White's fate.

**36 exf6 gxf6 37 ♔g1 ♔f7 38 ♔f2 ♔g6 39 ♔e2 ♔f5 40 g3 ♔e5 41 ♔f2 d4 42 g4 ♔d5 43 ♔e2 e5 44 ♔f2 e4 45 fxe4+ ♔xe4 46 ♖e2+ ♖e3 47 ♖c2 ♖xh3 48 ♖c4 ♖h2+ 49 ♔g3 ♖xb2 50 ♖xa4 ♖b6 51 ♖b4 ♖a6 52 a4 ♔e3 53 a5 ♖xa5 54 ♖b6 h5 55 ♖e6+ ♔d2 56 gxh5 ♖xh5 57 ♖xf6 ♖e5 58 ♔f2 d3 59 ♔f1 ♔d1 60 ♔f2 d2 0-1**

### Grivas – Himmel
*Corfu 1991*

**1 d4 ♘f6 2 ♘f3 g6 3 c4 ♗g7 4 ♘c3 d5 5 ♗g5 ♘e4 6 ♗h4 ♘xc3 7 bxc3 c5 8 cxd5 ♕xd5 9 e3 ♘c6 10 ♗e2 cxd4 11 cxd4 ♕a5+ 12 ♕d2 ♕xd2+?**

Black surrenders the initiative on the queenside. His play was much better in Grivas-Malishauskas, Debrecen Echt 1992: 12...♗e6! 13 ♖b1! ♕xa2 14 ♕xa2 ♗xa2 15 ♖xb7 ♗d5 16 ♗b5 0-0 17 ♖d7 ♗xf3 18 gxf3 ♖ab8 19 ♗d3 e6 20 0-0 ♘b4 21 ♗e2 a5 22 ♖a1 ♘c2 23 ♖xa5 ♖b1+ 24 ♔g2 ♖b2 25 ♔f1 ♖b1+ 26 ♔g2 ♖b2 ½-½. White can improve his play and retain a slight plus.

**13 ♔xd2 a6 14 ♖ab1! e6 15 ♖hc1!** *(D)*

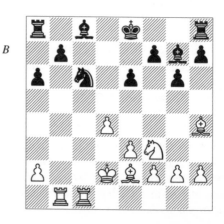

White already enjoys a significant superiority thanks to his better development, good central control and play on the b- and c-files. The semi-open b-file particularly troubles Black, since it prevents him from completing his development.

**15...h6 16 ♘e1!**

A very strong move, preparing ♘d3-c5 and ♗f3 to increase the pressure on the queenside. Black has no satisfactory defence and will soon lose material.

**16...0-0 17 ♘d3 ♖e8 18 ♗f3 (D)**

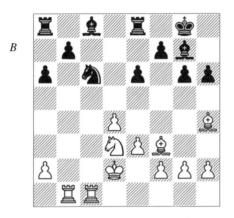

**18...e5**

An interesting try, since any passive move would suit White. However, White's position is so good that with some care he can force material gains and win the game without much effort.

**19 ♖xc6! e4 20 ♖c7 exf3 21 gxf3 ♗e6 22 ♖bxb7 ♗xa2 23 ♘b4! ♗b3 24 ♘xa6! ♗d5 25 ♖a7 ♖xa7 26 ♖xa7 ♗xf3 27 ♗g3**

The ending is easily winning.

**27....♗f8 28 ♘c7 ♖d8 29 ♔c3 g5 30 ♗e5 ♗e4 31 ♔c4 ♔h7 32 d5 ♔g6 33 ♔d4 ♗f3 34 ♖a6+ ♔h5 35 ♖f6 g4 36 ♖xf7 ♗a3 37 ♔c4 1-0**

### Kostopoulos – Grivas
*Athens 1991*

**1 f4 c5 2 b3 ♘f6 3 ♗b2 e6 4 ♘f3 ♗e7 5 e3 b6 6 ♗e2 ♗b7 7 0-0 0-0 8 ♘e5 (D)**

Without any particular ambition. A more natural continuation is 8 d3 and 9 ♘bd2, completing development.

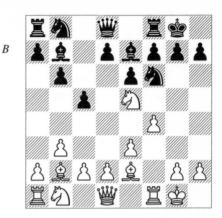

**8...d6 9 ♗f3 ♕c7 10 ♗xb7 ♕xb7 11 ♘g4 ♘bd7 12 ♘xf6+ ♗xf6 13 ♗xf6 ♘xf6**

Black has gladly accepted all exchanges proposed by White, as they helped him to complete his development harmoniously, without being troubled in the opening. The game effectively starts only at this point, since both sides are now compelled to come up with intricate strategic and tactical plans.

**14 d3 ♖fe8 15 e4?!**

The immediate 15 ♘d2 had to be played.

**15...e5! 16 c4**

After 16 f5? d5! Black is better, especially thanks to his control of the d-file that is about to open. But now 17 f5 is threatened.

**16...exf4 17 ♖xf4 ♕e7! 18 ♘a3 ♘d7 19 ♘b5 ♘f8 20 ♖f5 ♘e6 21 ♘c3 ♘d4 22 ♘d5 ♕d8 (D)**

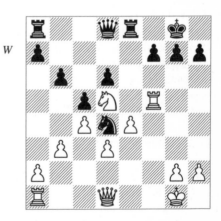

Both sides have placed their knights on their respective outposts, while also possessing one semi-open file each: White has the f-file, Black

the e-file. Is this position drawn after all? The
answer is no, and the key to this evaluation lies
on the placement of the white e-pawn and the
black f-pawn. Black has at his disposal one
more outpost, the e5-square, which he can use
as a transfer base for his pieces, including the
king in the endgame. Therefore, the semi-open
e-file is of greater importance than the f-file,
controlled by White. Even though these advantages may be considered infinitesimal, a good
chess-player can extract significant benefits by
exploiting them with proper technique.

**23 ♖f2 ♖e5! 24 ♕g4 ♖g5 25 ♕f4 f6 26 ♖af1
♘e6 27 ♕d2 ♖e5 28 ♘e3 ♘d4 29 ♘d5 ♔h8**
*(D)*

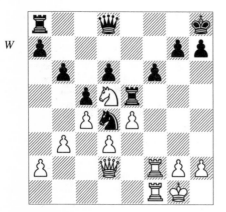

Black takes his time as White cannot develop any activity.

**30 ♘c3 ♕d7 31 ♘e2?!**

The exchange of knights is to Black's benefit, as White 'loses' a piece which could potentially create threats. White's problem is that he
doesn't believe he can lose this position and
thus doesn't worry at all.

**31...♘xe2+ 32 ♕xe2 ♖ae8 33 a4 ♔g8 34
♕d1 a6!**

Black entertains the thought of a future break
with ...b5.

**35 h3 ♕e6 36 ♖f5 ♖a8 37 ♕a1 ♕e8 38
♖5f2 ♖g5 39 ♖a2 ♕g6 40 ♖f3 ♖g3!** *(D)*

The exchange of one pair of rooks (or even
the queens as well) will allow the black king to
approach the centre. From there, with the help
of the proper breakthrough, he will be able to
dictate matters.

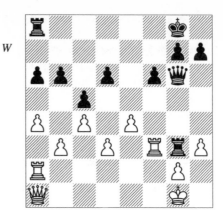

**41 ♕f1 ♕g5 42 ♖xg3 ♕xg3 43 ♕d1 ♖e8 44
♖f2 ♕e3 45 ♕d2 ♕d4 46 ♔h2 ♖e5**

It is now obvious that Black is making much
better use of his outposts on d4 and e5 than
White did with d5. The absence of any tactical
variations is also striking, as the game revolves
entirely around positional elements – boring
perhaps, but very significant.

**47 g3 ♔f7 48 ♔g2 ♔e7 49 ♕c2 ♔d7 50
♕d2 ♔c7**

The black king prepares to take part in the
proceedings!

**51 a5** *(D)*

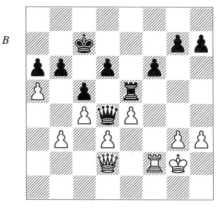

**51...♕a1!**

51...b5? would be a serious mistake, as then
the black king is deprived of an invasion path
on the queenside.

**52 axb6+ ♔xb6 53 b4 ♔c7 54 ♕a2?**

Black was of course better, but the road to victory was long and uncertain. With the exchange

of queens White's position becomes more vulnerable.

**54...♕xa2 55 ♖xa2 ♔b6 56 bxc5+ dxc5 57 ♔f3 ♖e7** *(D)*

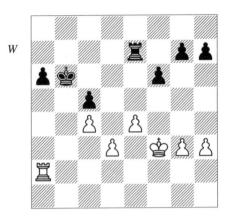

The essential difference between the respective pawn-structures, i.e. the passed black a6-pawn compared to the backward white d3-pawn, determines Black's advantage. The rook ending that has arisen offers White only very slight chances for survival. Black rushes to place his rook behind the passed pawn, thus freeing his king.

**58 g4 a5 59 ♔e3 ♖a7 60 ♖a4 ♔c6 61 d4**

In case White refrains from this move, Black will place his king on e5 and will eventually enter on d4, as White will lack any waiting moves.

**61...cxd4+ 62 ♔xd4 ♔d6!** *(D)*

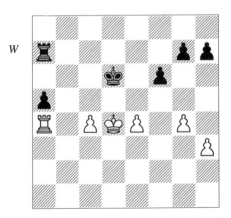

The pawn-structures have changed, but the essence of the position has not. The black a-

pawn is stronger than the white c-pawn (it is more distant), while the respective placement of the rooks is also in Black's favour. The win is in sight.

**63 c5+ ♔c6 64 ♔c4 ♖a8! 65 ♖a1 a4 66 ♖a3 ♖e8! 67 ♔d4 ♔b5 68 ♔d5 ♖d8+! 69 ♔e6 ♖c8 70 ♔d6 ♖c6+! 0-1**

## Botsari – Grivas
*Corfu 1993*

**1 d4 ♘f6 2 c4 g6 3 ♘c3 ♗g7 4 e4 d6 5 f3 a6 6 ♗g5 c6 7 ♕d2 b5 8 cxb5?!**

The theoretical 8 0-0-0 ♕a5 is surely better. The plan that White follows is rather prospectless.

**8...axb5 9 b4** *(D)*

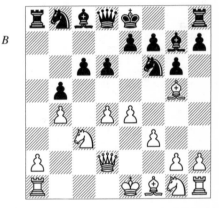

White has nailed down the backward c-pawn on the semi-open c-file, but is unlikely to be able to attack it or in any other way exploit the file. On the other hand, Black has been handed the semi-open a-file as well as an outpost on c4. Naturally, Black can be quite satisfied by the outcome of the opening.

**9...0-0 10 ♗d3 ♘bd7 11 ♘ge2**

In my opinion White should prefer the interesting 11 a4!? bxa4 12 ♖xa4 ♖xa4 13 ♘xa4 ♘b6! 14 ♘xb6 ♕xb6 15 ♘e2 ♗a6 16 ♗xa6 ♕xa6 17 0-0 ♖a8 18 ♖c1 with approximately equal chances.

**11...♘b6 12 0-0 ♗e6 13 f4**

White refuses to sit and wait, and correctly creates the preconditions for an attack against the black king. Regardless of whether the attack will prove successful or not, this operation is necessary from a practical point of view.

**13...&c4! 14 f5 &xd3 15 ♕xd3 &a3! 16 &c1 &a6 17 ♕h3 ♘a4!** (D)

W

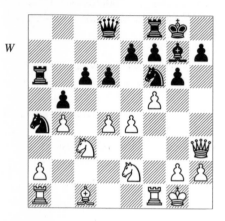

The correct reaction. Piece exchanges will weaken White's attacking prowess while at the same time highlighting her weaknesses. The outpost on c4 can wait, as piece exchanges and the exploitation of the a-file are of greater significance at the moment.

**18 &h1 ♘xc3 19 ♘xc3 ♘d7 20 &e3 &a3 21 &c1 &a6 22 &e3 ♘b6 23 &ad1** (D)

B

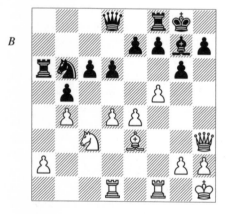

**23...♘a4!**

With the same idea as on the 17th move.

**24 ♘xa4**

White decides to 'forget' about the queenside pawns, as the variation 24 ♘e2 ♘b2! 25 &a1 ♘c4 is unattractive.

**24...&xa4 25 &h6 &xb4 26 e5 f6!** (D)

W

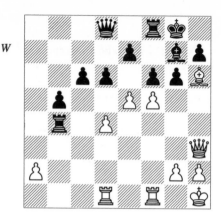

Again the correct decision. Black must focus on surviving White's attack, as otherwise all the positional benefits he has extracted will go to waste. From now on material gain is no longer important – it is only correct defence that counts.

**27 fxg6 hxg6 28 &f4**

Black also survives after 28 e6 f5! 29 &f4 ♕c8!.

**28...dxe5 29 &h4 &xh6?**

Black should play 29...g5! 30 &xg7 gxh4 31 &xf8 &xd4! 32 &f1 &xf8 winning.

**30 &xh6 &xd4 31 &h8+?**

White returns the favour! 31 &xd4! ♕xd4 (31...exd4?? 32 &h7 ♕a5 {else ♕h6} 33 &xe7 +–) 32 &h8+ &f7 33 &h7+ &e8 34 ♕c8+ ♕d8 35 ♕xc6+ draws.

**31...&f7 32 &h7+ &e8 33 &xd4 exd4 34 ♕g4** (D)

B

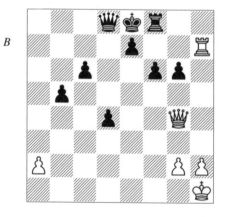

**34...♕d7!**

Pawns are less important than the safety of Black's king. Therefore, Black's only concern now is to transfer his king to a safe spot – without surrendering his entire material plus in the process, of course.

**35 ♕xg6+ ♔d8 36 ♖h3 ♕e6!**

Black's defence has succeeded and now his material superiority determines the outcome.

**37 ♕g3 ♔c8 38 ♕f2 ♖d8 39 ♖a3 ♔b7 40 ♕d2 ♕e4 41 h3 ♖g8 42 ♖f3 c5 0-1**

## Orfanos – Grivas
*Aegina 1996*

**1 d4 ♘f6 2 c4 g6 3 ♘c3 ♗g7 4 e4 d6 5 f3 a6 6 ♗e3 c6 7 ♕d2 b5 8 cxb5 axb5 9 b4 0-0 10 ♗d3 ♘bd7 11 ♘ge2 ♘b6 12 0-0 ♗e6 13 ♗h6**

White repeated the same mistake as in the previous game. Here he chooses a different route on the 13th move (the only difference is the placement of the bishop on e3, instead of g5 as in the previous game).

**13...♗c4!**

Exchanging the bishop that controls the c4-square, thus paving the way for the b6-knight to occupy it.

**14 ♗xc4 ♘xc4 15 ♕g5 ♖a3!**

Commencing operations on the semi-open a-file.

**16 ♔h1** *(D)*

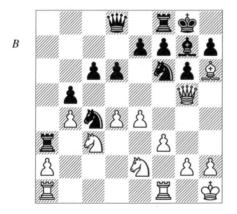

**16...d5!?**

An interesting idea, solidifying the position of the c4-knight and intending to block the advance of White's central pawns.

**17 e5 ♘d7 18 ♕h4 ♗xh6 19 ♕xh6 e6**

Black keeps the white pawns in check, while the a-file can wait.

**20 ♖ac1 ♕e7 21 ♖b1**

It becomes clear that White is at a loss for a plan and decides to bide his time; this approach is almost always detrimental.

**21...f6!**

Black opens a second front, at the same time extinguishing any potential white initiative on the kingside. The weak backward e6-pawn is in no danger whatsoever, as the white pieces cannot coordinate against it.

**22 exf6 ♕xf6 23 ♖b3 ♖a7!** *(D)*

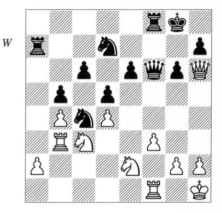

The b3-rook is probably White's worst piece and Black must not allow its exchange. The a7-rook combines activity on the semi-open a-file with defensive duties along its 2nd rank.

**24 ♖d1**

24 f4 ♘d2 is even worse for White.

**24...e5!**

Black now adds another to his collection of advantages: a passed d-pawn.

**25 ♕c1 ♕h4 26 dxe5 ♘dxe5**

Black is winning. He has strong pressure on the semi-open a-file (tying down White's pieces to its protection), a passed d-pawn, good piece coordination and attacking chances against the white king.

**27 ♘d4 ♕f2 28 ♖b1 ♖e7 29 ♕h6 ♘e3 30 ♖g1 ♘3g4 31 fxg4 ♕xd4 32 ♘e2 0-1**

White lost on time before Black had the chance to continue with 32...♘xg4! 33 ♕xf8+ ♔xf8 34 ♖gf1+ ♘f2+!.

# Forepost

The strategic element of the forepost is directly related to those of the open file and the outpost. From this one can deduce the actual definition of the term (which is here being introduced into English-language chess literature), i.e. an outpost on an open file, on which we can place a minor piece.

But what is the use of the forepost? Why is it so important?

With the use of the forepost we achieve the blocking of a file that we are not immediately able to control. Behind the forepost we can double our rooks or manoeuvre them with complete freedom. At an appropriate moment the forepost can be removed, allowing our rooks to spring into action. If necessary, the file can be blocked again in the same way.

The piece occupying the forepost may simultaneously be able to create threats, so that the opponent is unable to fulfil all defensive requirements of his position and allow the invasion of our rooks.

In general, the combination of an open file, a forepost and an outpost is a significant strategic advantage in itself and may easily suffice for victory.

In certain rare cases the forepost may be used on diagonals that need to be blocked, utilizing the same mechanism.

## Komljenović – Grivas
*Munich 1987*

**1 d4 f5 2 ♘f3 ♘f6 3 g3 g6 4 ♗g2 ♗g7 5 0-0 0-0 6 c4 d6 7 ♘c3 ♕e8 8 d5 ♘a6 9 ♗e3**

A new continuation that doesn't trouble Black. White's main options in this position are 9 ♘d4 and 9 ♖b1.

**9...c6 10 ♖b1**

10 ♖c1 and 10 ♕b3 are also possible, and more in the spirit of the position.

**10...♗d7 11 ♕d2?!** *(D)*

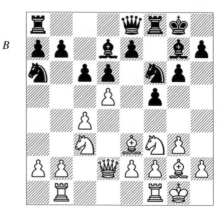

B

It becomes evident that White is not operating on the basis of a specific plan but is just making some 'simple' moves. This approach cannot bring any positive results.

**11...♘g4! 12 ♗d4 ♗h6!**

This had escaped White's attention. The next few moves are forced.

**13 ♘g5 c5 14 ♗e3 ♘xe3 15 ♕xe3 ♘c7** *(D)*

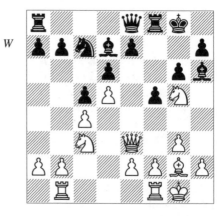

W

Black has obtained the bishop-pair and his position strikes one as more harmonious in general. His immediate plan is to start play on the queenside. The only plan apparently available to White is the advance e4, which requires a lot of preparatory moves (h4, f4, ♕d3); still, it is his only decent plan.

**16 b4?**

As mentioned above, this cannot be the right idea. With this move White further weakens his dark squares and offers Black the semi-open c-file, with a ready-made target on it (the c4-pawn).

**16...cxb4 17 ♖xb4 b6 18 ♕f4 ♘a6 19 ♖bb1 ♖c8! 20 ♘b5**

The only way to avoid material losses. Black had of course foreseen this continuation and now proceeds to transform his advantage: the strategic advantages of the semi-open file and the backward c-pawn are exchanged for an open file and a better minor piece (knight vs bishop).

**20...♗xb5! 21 cxb5 ♘c5 22 ♕h4 ♗xg5 23 ♕xg5** *(D)*

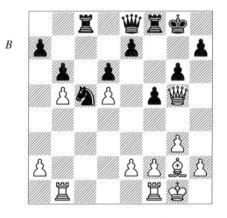

Black is better, mainly thanks to his excellent knight. On c5, this knight is fulfilling an important task, that of Black's forepost on the c-file. Black is planning to improve the placement of his queen at first and then to double his rooks on the c-file, awaiting a suitable moment to move the c5-knight and occupy the file. White's greatest cause for headaches is the passivity of his position.

**23...♕f7! 24 ♖b4 ♕f6! 25 ♕d2**

After 25 ♕xf6 exf6! Black would also enjoy possession of the semi-open e-file. On the other hand, the black queen is now dominantly placed on the long a1-h8 diagonal, controlling several important squares.

**25...♖c7!** *(D)*

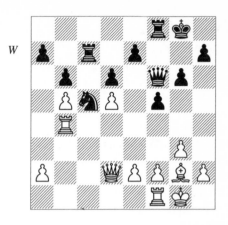

**26 ♖c4??**

White fails to withstand the pressure. The correct move-order was 26 ♖c1 ♖fc8 27 ♖bc4, when Black is better but the conversion of his advantage into victory will require hard work.

**26...♘e4! 27 ♕c2 ♖xc4 28 ♕xc4 ♘d2 0-1**

**Grivas – P. Genov**
*Iraklion 1993*

**1 d4 ♘f6 2 c4 e6 3 ♘f3 b6 4 g3 ♗a6 5 ♕b3 c6?!**

5...♘c6 remains the main line.

**6 ♗g5!**

The automatic 6 ♗g2 d5 would fully justify Black's last move. Since the h1-a8 diagonal will be blocked after ...d5, the white bishop will have no targets on g2.

**6...d5** *(D)*

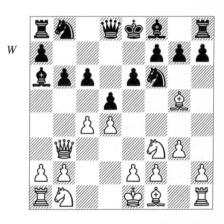

**7 cxd5! cxd5**

7...exd5?! 8 ♗xf6! ♕xf6 9 ♘c3 ♘d7 10 ♗g2 followed by 0-0, ♖fe1 and e4 promises a clear advantage to White.

**8 e3! ♗xf1 9 ♔xf1 ♗e7 10 ♔g2 ♘c6!**

The only continuation so as not to lose control of the c-file. After 10...♘bd7?! 11 ♖c1 0-0 12 ♘c3 a6 13 ♘a4 Black's problems would be insoluble.

**11 ♖c1 ♘a5 12 ♕b5+! ♕d7 13 ♕a6!**

Threatening 14 ♘e5!.

**13...♗d6 14 ♗xf6 gxf6 15 ♘c3 ♕b7 16 ♕e2**

The exchange of queens would significantly relieve Black (16 ♕xb7? ♘xb7 17 ♘b5 ♔d7!), who now faces a multitude of problems: not only must he cater for the c-file, but also for his kingside weaknesses.

**16...0-0 17 ♖c2!** *(D)*

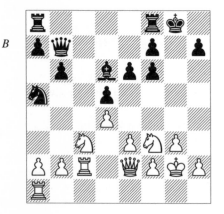

What we practically have here is a case of a forepost (the c3-knight) very close to the white camp. White will double rooks on the c-file and at the same time develop an initiative on the flank where the exposed black king resides. At the appropriate moment the forepost will be removed in such a way that Black will be unable to defend against all of White's threats. A simple plan, but the execution is difficult!

**17...♖ac8 18 ♖ac1 ♔g7 19 ♘e1!**

A strong move, aiming at the transfer of the knight(s) to the f4-square; from there, in combination with the approach of the white queen (♕h5) they will be able to create direct threats against the black king.

**19...f5 20 ♘d3 ♘c4?!** *(D)*

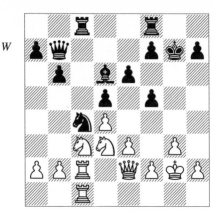

This appears strong, but in reality only serves to complicate Black's defensive task, as this knight works as a second forepost for White. Better is 20...♘c6 and ...♘e7, assigning the knight to the defence of the king.

**21 ♕h5 h6 22 ♘e2! ♕a6?**

With the false impression of imminent material gain, thanks to the double threat 23...♕xa2 and 23...♘xe3+. The defensive 22...♕d7 was essential.

**23 ♘ef4!** *(D)*

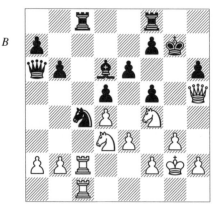

**23...♗e7**

23...♕xa2 is no improvement: 24 ♕h4! ♖c7 25 ♘h5+ ♔h7 26 ♘f6+ ♔g7 27 ♘f4! ♖fc8 (27...♗xf4 28 gxf4 intending ♖g1 and ♔h3+) 28 ♔h1! ♗e7 29 g4!.

**24 b3 ♘d6 25 ♘e5! ♗g5** *(D)*

This move loses in spectacular fashion, but anyway there was no salvation. Black could not free his position by 25...♖xc2 26 ♖xc2 ♖c8 in

view of 27 ♘xf7 ♘xf7 (27...♖xc2 28 ♕g6+
♔f8 29 ♘xe6+ ♔e8 30 ♘e5+!) 28 ♕g6+ ♔f8
(28...♔h8 29 ♖xc8+ ♕xc8 30 ♕xf7) 29 ♘xe6+
♔e8 30 ♖c7!, winning for White.

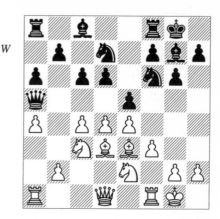

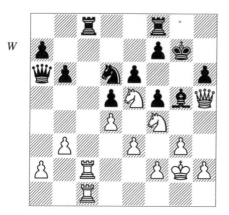

**26 ♘xe6+!!**

White's great positional superiority creates
the basic requirements for tactical combinations.

**26...fxe6 27 ♖c7+ ♔h8 28 ♕g6 1-0**

Black cannot avoid checkmate.

### Grivas – Kolani

*Ankara 1993*

**1 d4 d6 2 e4 ♘f6 3 f3 g6 4 ♗e3 c6 5 c4 ♘bd7 6
♘c3 a6?! 7 a4!**

Black has already developed the queen's
knight to d7, so he does not have the usual manoeuvre ...♘a6-b4 at his disposal after 7...a5.

**7...♕a5 8 ♗d3 ♗g7 9 ♘ge2 0-0 10 0-0 e5**
*(D)*

**11 ♖b1!**

Preparing to meet 11...c5 with 12 b4! cxb4
13 ♘a2. Similarly, after 11...exd4 12 b4! White
would have the edge.

**11...♕c7 12 ♕d2 ♖e8 13 b4 b6 14 b5**

Fighting for control of the d5-square. Black
has no choice.

**14...axb5 15 axb5 c5 16 d5**

After 16 dxe5 ♘xe5! Black has adequate
counterplay.

**16...♗b7 17 ♖a1 ♘f8?!**

The direct 17...♖xa1 18 ♖xa1 ♖a8 seems
better. White would retain a plus thanks to his

space advantage and kingside attacking potential, but Black would in turn have partly got rid
of his problems on the a-file.

**18 ♕b2 ♘6d7 19 g3 f6 20 ♘a4!** *(D)*

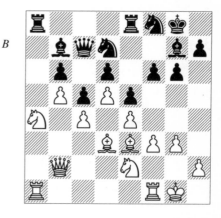

White uses the a4-knight as a forepost. His
spatial superiority allows him to develop an initiative on both sides of the board but, for this
venture to prove successful, he must refrain
from exchanging pieces; this would help Black,
who is suffering from a lack of space.

**20...♖a7 21 ♖a2 ♖ea8 22 ♖fa1 ♕b8 23 ♗d2**

As Black can only wait, White improves the
placement of his pieces in preparation for the f4
break, which anyway is the only really promising idea at his disposal.

**23...♔f7 24 ♕c2 ♔g8 25 ♘c1 ♕d8 26 ♗f1
♔f7 27 ♗h3 ♕b8 28 ♘d3 ♕d8 29 ♖e1 ♗c8 30
♖ea1 ♗b7 31 ♖f1 ♗c8 32 f4**

After several preparatory moves White proceeds according to plan.

**32...♔g8 33 ♖a3 ♔h8 34 fxe5**

Another good option was 34 f5 g5 35 ♗g4! intending h4, ♔g2 and ♖h1.

**34...♘xe5 35 ♘xe5 dxe5**

This move offers White a passed d-pawn, but 35...fxe5 36 ♗xc8 ♖xc8 37 ♖af3 is too dangerous to contemplate.

**36 ♗xc8 ♖xc8 37 ♖fa1 ♖ca8 38 ♕b3 ♘d7** *(D)*

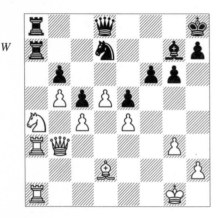

If Black could place his knight on d6 he wouldn't face any real problems. However, things are not that simple.

**39 ♘c3!**

The time has come to remove the forepost, since White has, thanks to his purposeful strategy, increased his advantage (in addition to his spatial plus, better bishop and forepost he now also has a protected passed pawn). Naturally, the white rooks will not manage to infiltrate into the enemy camp as they will be promptly exchanged. However, the occupation of the a-file by the white queen will prove just as significant, in combination with the advance of the white pawns on the kingside (minority attack!), and will further increase White's plus.

**39...♖xa3 40 ♖xa3 ♖xa3 41 ♕xa3 ♕b8 42 g4!**

Preventing a possible pawn-break with ...f5, while also clearing the g3-square for the knight, which can help the advance of the kingside pawns. Indeed, the advances g5 and h4-h5 are an integral part of White's plan, since he cannot hope to win only on one flank but needs to combine play on both.

**42...h6 43 ♘e2 ♔h7 44 ♘g3 ♘f8 45 ♕a6 ♘d7 46 h4!** *(D)*

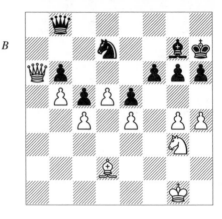

White now threatens 47 h5, gaining the f5-square for his knight. White's superiority would be clear, perhaps even decisive, but Black anyway had to sit tight. The sacrifice he now employs offers nothing of value and hence should have been avoided.

**46...f5? 47 gxf5 ♘f6 48 fxg6+ ♔xg6 49 ♔g2 ♔h7 50 ♕a3!**

The queen's mission on the a-file has ended, as new and more significant inroads have been created on the kingside.

**50...♘e8 51 ♘f5 ♘d6 52 ♕g3 ♕f8 53 ♘xd6 ♕xd6 54 h5 ♕f6 55 ♕g4 ♔g8 56 ♗e1 ♕d8 57 ♗g3 ♕f6 58 ♕f5 ♕xf5 59 exf5 e4 1-0**

### Grivas – Gabriel
*Budapest 1994*

**1 d4 d5 2 c4 e6 3 ♘f3 ♘f6 4 ♘c3 ♗e7 5 ♗g5 0-0 6 e3 h6 7 ♗h4 b6 8 ♗d3 dxc4**

This move is not considered the most accurate. 8...♗b7 9 0-0 ♘bd7 10 ♕e2 ♘e4 lends a more dynamic character to the position.

**9 ♗xc4 ♗b7 10 0-0 ♘bd7 11 ♕e2** *(D)* **11...♘e4**

Black is trying to free his position by exchanges. Instead, the premature 11...c5?! 12 ♖fd1 would be fraught with danger for Black.

**12 ♘xe4 ♗xe4**

After the alternative 12...♗xh4 13 ♘c3! ♗f6 14 ♖fd1 ♕e7 15 ♗a6! White is in the driving seat.

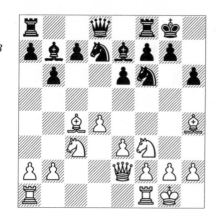

*B*

**13 ♗g3! ♗d6 14 ♖fd1 ♗xg3 15 hxg3 ♕e7 16 ♖ac1 ♖fd8 17 ♗d3!**

Both sides have played useful moves, preparing for the eventual ...c5 advance.

**17...♗xd3 18 ♖xd3 c5 19 ♖dc3! ♘f6?**

Black should refrain from releasing the tension and wait with 19...a5 20 ♕b5 ♖ab8.

**20 dxc5! ♘e4 21 ♖c4 ♘xc5 22 ♘d4! ♕f8 23 b4! ♘d7 24 ♘c6 ♖e8** *(D)*

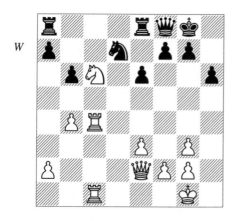

*W*

White's superiority is obvious. He controls the c-file while the c6-knight (the forepost) radiates power. Moreover, the black pieces are huddled on the back rank, devoid of any prospects.

**25 e4 ♘f6 26 ♖d1?!**

There was no reason for this move. Much better was 26 a4! or even 26 ♖4c3 and ♖a3.

**26...b5!? 27 ♖c5 a6 28 ♕c2?!**

White has strayed from the right path. After 28 a4! bxa4 29 ♕c4 he would retain his advantage.

**28...♔h8 29 ♘e5 ♔g8 30 ♘c6 ♔h8 31 a3 ♖ec8 32 ♘e5?!** *(D)*

From the 26th move onwards White has been playing without a particular plan of converting his superiority. Consequently, he slowly ruins his position. 32 f3 and 33 ♖c1 was necessary.

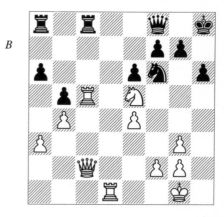

*B*

**32...♖xc5 33 bxc5 ♖c8 34 c6 ♕e7 35 ♔h1?!**

White should of course continue 35 f3! ♕c7 36 ♕c3, when he retains the better chances, despite the childish mistakes committed so far.

**35...♔g8! 36 a4 b4 37 ♕c4 a5 38 f4 ♕c7 39 ♖d3 ♕b6 40 ♔h2 h5 41 ♕b5 ♕c7 42 ♖d4 ½-½**

White could continue pressing for victory, but instead agreed to a draw, disappointed with his many mistakes.

### I. Nikolaidis – Grivas
*Karditsa 1998*

**1 d4 ♘f6 2 c4 g6 3 g3 ♗g7 4 ♗g2 0-0 5 ♘f3 d6 6 0-0 ♘c6 7 ♘c3 ♗f5 8 ♗g5 ♘e4?!**

A mediocre reaction to a rather mediocre line (8 ♗g5). 8...h6 9 ♗xf6 ♗xf6 is preferable.

**9 ♘xe4 ♗xe4 10 d5 ♗xf3?**

Black fails to understand the problems of the position. 10...♘b8 should be preferred.

**11 exf3!** *(D)*

Intending to apply pressure on the semi-open e-file and the backward e7-pawn in particular.

**11...♘e5 12 ♖c1 b6?!**

The immediate 12...♗f6 is better. Black mistakenly feared White's c5 advance.

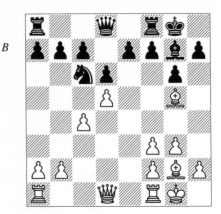

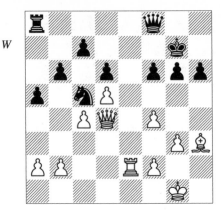

**13 Re1 Bf6 14 h4!**

Naturally, 14 Bxf6? exf6 would immediately solve Black's problems.

**14...a5 15 f4! Nd7 16 Re2!**

Black's position is already lost. White threatens to double rooks on the e-file and place his light-squared bishop on h3, while Black is devoid of any substantial prospects.

**16...Nc5 17 Bh3 Kg7 18 h5 h6**

Ugly, but what else is there?

**19 Bxf6+ exf6 20 Qd4!**

If Black were given time to play 20...f5, shutting out the white bishop, a great part of his difficulties would vanish.

**20...Re8 21 Rce1 Rxe2 22 Rxe2 Qf8 23 hxg6 fxg6?** *(D)*

Black's only chance lay in 23...Re8! 24 Rxe8 Qxe8 25 gxf7 Kxf7, retaining some survival chances despite the material deficit.

**24 Be6!**

The forepost! Now the black rook will be aimlessly moving to and fro, while White will have all the time in the world to organize his future plans.

**24...Re8 25 Re3 Re7 26 f5 g5?**

The last error. 26...gxf5 27 Qf4 Kh8 was essential.

**27 b3! Qe8 28 a3 Nd7 29 Bxd7! Qxd7 30 Re6! Rf7** *(D)*

No better is 30...Rxe6 31 fxe6 Qe7 32 g4!. White will bring his king to f5 and then advance his queenside pawns, while in the meantime Black will run out of useful moves.

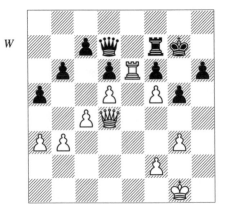

**31 Qd1! Rf8 32 Qe2! 1-0**

Black resigned due to 32...Rf7 33 Qh5!. A very 'clean' game, despite (or rather thanks to!) Black's mistakes, where several strategic elements were encountered: open and semi-open files, forepost and passed pawn!

# Index of Games

## List of Efstratios Grivas's Opponents

Numbers refer to pages. When a page number appears in **bold**, Grivas had White. Otherwise his opponent had White.

| | |
|---|---|
| Agnos | 47 |
| Annageldiev | 59 |
| Arlandi | 92 |
| Blatny | **73** |
| Botsari | 99 |
| Bousios | 95 |
| Bras | 69 |
| Buckley, G. | 57 |
| Cheparinov | 55 |
| Collin | 23 |
| Conquest | 58 |
| Dedes | 49 |
| Espinosa Flores | **64** |
| Gabriel | **106** |
| Gelfand | 33 |
| Genov, P. | **103** |
| Georgadze, G. | **37** |
| Goldberg | **75** |
| Gotsche | 81 |
| Halldorsson | **71** |
| Haritakis | **72** |
| Hebden | 27 |
| Himmel | **96** |
| Hornung | **79** |
| Karanikolas, K. | **83** |
| Kjeldsen | **13** |
| Kolani | **105** |
| Komljenović | 102 |
| Koskinen | **85** |
| Kostopoulos | 97 |
| Kotronias | **19**, 39 |
| Lagopatis | **17** |
| Likavsky | 86 |
| Lputian | **42** |
| Lukacs | 34 |
| Makropoulos | 31 |

| | |
|---|---|
| Malakhatko | 53 |
| Minasian, Art. | 44 |
| Movsesian | 45 |
| Nikolaidis, I. | 107 |
| Nunn | **87** |
| Orfanos | 101 |
| Pandavos, P. | **88** |
| Pinter | **51** |
| Polgar, J. | **41** |
| Polgar, Zsu. | **66** |
| Popović | **63** |
| Radulov | **61** |
| Roiz | 76 |
| Siebrecht | **16** |
| Simić, R. | **82** |
| Skembris | **28** |
| Soylu | 90 |
| Stipić | **30** |
| Stoica | 93 |
| Szkudlarek | **15** |
| Vajda, A. | **77** |
| Velikov | **36**, 67 |
| Vouldis | 24, 25 |
| Wells | 21 |
| Yrjölä | 89 |

## Other Game

| | |
|---|---|
| Apicella – Svidler | 75 |

# Index of Openings

Numbers refer to pages. Codes are ECO codes.

**Flank Openings**
A02 *97*; A08 *31*; A09 *36, 58*

**English Opening**
A10 *15*; A13 *72*; A29 *75*

**Queen's Pawn Misc.**
A56 *79*; A57 *13*

**Modern Benoni**
A68 *30, 57*; A69 *55*; A71 *19*

**Dutch Defence**
A82 *81*; A87 *102*; A94 *71*

**Pirc Defence**
B07 *17, 105*

**Sicilian Defence**
B33 *24, 25, 39, 44, 45, 49*; B51 *21, 90*; B70 *75*; B82 *47*

**French Defence**
C02 *95*

**1 e4 e5 Misc.**
C36 *27*; C55 *93*

**Ruy Lopez (Spanish)**
C82 *23*

**1 d4 d5 Misc.**
D03 *73*

**Queen's Gambit**
D15 *16*; D21 *66*; D24 *64*; D44 *51*; D45 *85*; D58 *83, 106*; D63 *88*

**Grünfeld Defence**
D91 *42, 63, 82, 96*; D94 *61*

**Queen's Indian Defence**
E15 *103*

**Nimzo-Indian Defence**
E31 *28*; E40 *37*

**King's Indian Defence**
E62 *107*; E68 *67*; E71 *41, 87*; E80 *99, 101*; E90 *92*; E92 *59, 76*; E94 *69, 77, 86*; E97 *33, 53, 89*; E99 *34*

## 50 Essential Chess Lessons
*Steve Giddins*
Many of these instructive games are unknown in Western literature. Russian-speaker Steve Giddins discusses the lessons to be learned, in a style refreshingly free of dogma.
*160 pages, 248 x 172 mm; $24.95 / £14.99*

## Understanding the Chess Openings
*Sam Collins*
This indispensable new one-volume reference work surveys *all* important chess openings. All main lines are covered, with typical strategies for both sides explained.
*224 pages, 248 x 172 mm; $28.95 / £16.99*

## Chess College 2: Pawn Play
*Efstratios Grivas*
This second volume in the series teaches all aspects of pawn play that are vital to successful chess. Topics include: isolated pawns, doubled pawns, backward pawns, hanging pawns, pawn majorities and minorities, and central strikes.
*112 pages, 248 x 172 mm; $19.95 / £12.99*

## Chess College 3: Technique
*Efstratios Grivas*
Great technique is the hallmark of champions. Topics include bishop vs knight, standard sacrifices against the castled enemy king, opposite-coloured bishops, and advice on how to handle won and lost positions.
*112 pages, 248 x 172 mm; $19.95 / £12.99*

## Secrets of Modern Chess Strategy
*John Watson*
"...can, without resorting to hyperbole, be considered a classic..." – GM Nigel Short, THE SUNDAY TELEGRAPH
*272 pages, 248 x 172 mm; $24.95 / £19.99*

## Chess Endgame Training
*Bernd Rosen*
An endgame course with a difference. While solving exercises requiring precise calculation, the reader learns much about general endgame strategy.
*176 pages, 210 x 145 mm; $19.95 / £13.99*

## Understanding Pawn Play in Chess
*Dražen Marović*
"An ideal study companion for an improving beginner or an average club player who wants to improve his/her handling of pawn structures" – Alan Sutton, EN PASSANT
*208 pages, 210 x 145 mm; $21.95 / £14.99*

## Beat the Grandmasters
*Christian Kongsted*
Imagine you are facing a grandmaster, and have a chance to find the winning combination. This book will test your skills with real-game situations.
*176 pages, 210 x 145 mm; $25.95 / £14.99*

## Chess Training for Budding Champions
*Jesper Hall*
This book is perfect for players who have acquired the basic skills to play at club level, and now need guidance to improve their overall understanding of chess.
*176 pages, 226 x 174 mm; $19.95 / £14.99*

## Learn Chess Tactics
*John Nunn*
"It is an orderly, methodical and very useful manual. Aimed not only at beginners, the book can open the tactical horizon to many tournament players." – GM Lubosh Kavalek, WASHINGTON POST
*160 pages, 248 x 172 mm; $19.95 / £12.99*

---

**About the Publisher**: Gambit is a chess publishing company run exclusively by chess masters and grandmasters. With over 140 chess books in print, there is an extensive selection of titles to assist intermediate-level players to improve. Gambit books are widely used in chess schools and chess camps as training material for students.

www.gambitbooks.com